The Lady From Hell

Memories of a WWII B-17 Top Turret Gunner

To Richard

I hope you enjoy my journey

Frank

Frank J. Condreras
Technical Sergeant
United States Army Eighth Air Force

Copyright © 2005 Frank J. Condreras

All rights reserved.

ISBN 1-4196-0556-9

To order additional copies, please contact us.
BookSurge, LLC
www.booksurge.com
1-866-308-6235
orders@booksurge.com

Table of Contents

Dedication	i
Introduction	ii
Prologue	iii
Brooklyn	1
The Bulletin	13
Graduation	19
The Induction	23
Fort Dix	29
Basic Training	37
Airplane Mechanic School	59
Aerial Gunnery School	73
At Last, A Furlough	83
Florida, The Second Time	91
Advanced Combat Training	101
Saying Goodbye to America	109
Hello! Chelveston	117
My First Mission	127
The Lady From Hell	151
Finally, The P-51s	161
Europe's Winter Weather	183
The Destruction Continues	199
Farewell to a Lady	211
Rescued by the Russians	221
The Long Trip Back to Base	239
Germany Surrenders	259
Heading Back to the U.S.A	271
The Discharge	283
A Civilian Again	293
The Changing Times	303

Getting Reacquainted	313
The Job Search	321
My New Life	335
Epilogue	345
About the Author	349

The Lady From Hell

DEDICATION

I would like to dedicate this book to all my friends who I met in the service, especially to my war buddies, with whom I flew in combat, and to the all too many of them who never returned...

...to the most beautiful airplane in the world, the B-17 Flying Fortress, particularly one we called "The Lady From Hell"...

...to the Russian infantry, who saved my life from the German army and the swamps of Poland...

...and last, but not least, to my three girls, whom I love very much: my wife, Mary, and my daughters, Susan and Linda.

Frank J. Condreras

INTRODUCTION

This is my story. It begins on December 7, 1941, on an early Sunday afternoon. It is a story written from over sixty years of memories, so some of the facts and figures relating to dates, times, and places may be a little inaccurate.

These are true stories. The names used in this book are fictitious, but they represent real friends, ranking officers, fellow soldiers, and other individuals who played important roles in my life.

The Lady From Hell

PROLOGUE

No one knew on the morning of March 17, 1945 that we would not return that afternoon. We had a restless night's sleep as we always did the night before a mission. We waited, with anxious anticipation, to board "The Lady From Hell." She was a B-17 Flying Fortress heavy bomber, and she was so named because she had brought us through hell and back many times. The target for that day was Jena, a city near Berlin, and it would be my twenty-seventh and final mission.

I was a nineteen-year-old flight engineer and top turret gunner for the United States Army Air Corp., and I worked on a remarkable airplane. I had arrived in Europe in early 1944, and Chelveston, England was to be my home until the end of the war, or until the end of my service. But, I'm getting ahead of my story; so let me start from the beginning...

1

BROOKLYN

Contrary to what you may have heard, Brooklyn, New York, was a beautiful place in which to grow up. I was born in Brooklyn, the oldest of three children. We lived in a two-family red brick house, which had six rooms, top and bottom, two beautiful porches, and a half-finished basement. My mom and dad, together with my grandfather, bought this home for the sum of two thousand, six hundred dollars. It was to become my home for twenty-eight years. Many happy memories were made in this house, and also some very sad ones.

I remember as a little boy, hearing about the stock market crash and of the terrible depression that followed. Many people lost their jobs because of the depression, including my grandfather. Thank God my dad was able to hold on to his job. It became his responsibility to feed two families and pay the mortgage. If you could not meet your mortgage payments, you could defer the principle until a later date, and just pay the interest. I do not remember whether this was a government order, or a decision by the banks themselves. This ruling was a Godsend for many homeowners, as it helped many people save their homes. Still, there were many who lost their homes. I remember people standing on corners selling apples for five cents, trying to make ends meet. These were dark and dreary days for the entire nation.

There were very few cars on the roads as I was growing up in Brooklyn. In fact, my entire block, which consisted of some thirty-six homes, had but six cars. I remember some of the older model cars had to be started by a hand crank. Someone would stand in front of the car and insert this crank into a hole underneath the radiator. The person then turned this crank as fast as possible, until the engine kicked over. The crank would then have to

The Lady From Hell

be pulled out quickly, or the person risked suffering a broken arm or wrist. Since most people worked six days a week, these cars were used only on Sundays to take the family out for a ride. Most deliveries were made by horse-drawn wagons. My dad was one of these deliverymen. He worked for a company known as Sheffield Farms, delivering milk, butter, and cheeses. I remember hearing him getting up at four o'clock in the morning, six days a week, for many years. The highlight of my day would be when he would pass by our house so he could give me a ride to school in his horse-drawn wagon, much to the envy of my friends. I owe a lot to my dad. He was a hard-working man who never complained. All through the depression, our family always ate three meals a day. Many families did not.

Frank J. Condreras

The wide streets and scarcity of cars made for plenty of room to play hockey and other sports in Brooklyn.

Most of the deliveries were made in the mornings, which left the streets clear the rest of the day so that we could play ball. Most of us believed Brooklyn was the ball playing capital of the world. Some of the best players came from Brooklyn. Growing up, we played all kinds of ball; stick ball, punch ball, box ball, and handball. We also roller-skated and played roller hockey in our streets. Brooklyn was still in its infancy, and not completely developed. There were many empty lots all over, which served as

The Lady From Hell

our football fields. The big games played between different neighborhoods were played in the schoolyards or public parks, usually under the supervision of the police.

In the winter, the snows came quite often and remained on the ground. There was no plowing, salting, or sanding, and there were very few cars. In those days, the snow remained where it fell, white and clean, practically all winter long. People would shovel their stoops and walks, throwing the snow to the curb, where it gradually formed huge mountains. As winter progressed, they would get higher and higher. Only a warming trend would reduce the size of these snow mountains. Many "King-of the-Hill" battles were fought on top of these snow mountains.

Whenever we had a snowstorm that measured six inches or more, the New York City Department of Sanitation would pay seventy-five cents an hour to anyone willing to clear the streets, thus allowing people to cross from one corner to another. During the depression, there was a lot of competition for these jobs. In fairness, the city would try to give these jobs to the married men with families who were unemployed. Eight hours of pay would give you six dollars, and in those days, it would be enough to feed a family for more than a week.

We younger kids also made out. We would go from house to house asking people if they would like their walk cleared. Depending on the size of the property, we would get anywhere from twenty-five to fifty cents. We would stop only because of the darkness. There would be a lot of aching muscles the next day, but it was well worth it. Whatever we made, we would bring home to our families.

The main modes of transportation for us "Brooklynites" were the subway and the trolley cars. For the tremendous sum of five cents, you could travel to the 1939 World's Fair, or to Yankee Stadium in the Bronx, or to Times Square in Manhattan. From where I lived, to go to Coney Island or Ebbett's Field, where our beloved Dodgers played, we would take the trolley cars. Our

The Lady From Hell

transportation system was clean, crime-free, and, most of the time, on schedule.

I cannot write about my beloved Brooklyn without mentioning our shopping habits. In the early 1930s, there were no supermarkets. Instead, we had "Mom and Pop" stores, which were small specialty stores. Instead of large markets, we had grocery stores, butcher shops, fruit and vegetable stores, and bakeries. Candy stores, drug stores, hardware stores, and clothing stores were usually small businesses owned and operated by families, and could be found on every block. Most of the owners of these stores lived in the back of the store, or in an apartment above the store. If some emergency arose, they would always be available.

There was no such thing as a refrigerator in these days. Instead, we had what was called an icebox. It had a door and several shelves. An iceman would deliver a block of ice in the morning, for ten cents, and place it on the bottom shelf. As the ice melted, the water would go into a drain, and end up in a large pan located underneath the icebox. It would be necessary to empty this pan several times a day to avoid a flood on the kitchen floor. As the day progressed, the ice block would get smaller and smaller, and the icebox would get warmer and warmer. It did not do its job very well, so shopping for perishable foods, such as meats, fish, fruits and vegetables, was an everyday chore. Saturday was the big shopping day, since we would be shopping for the weekend, and for any relatives and friends that would be coming for Sunday dinner.

In the afternoons on Sunday, the streets of Brooklyn were deserted. All stores were closed, with the exception of the candy store, which remained open until around noon to sell their newspapers. After Sunday services, most people stayed indoors to enjoy their dinners. On Sunday in my house, dinner was a feast. Our family would sit around the large dining room table, dinner would begin around one o'clock, and we would not stop eating until well into the evening. The day was spent eating, drinking, and telling jokes. Many times there would be several conversations going on at the same time, but everyone was happy, everyone had a good time, and everyone was feeling good. Yes, Sunday was a special day in our lives. On Monday morning, things would return to normal, as the streets would again bustle with people.

Holidays were something special. We were always lucky to have a Christmas tree, which the entire family took great delight in decorating. Each year we would proclaim, "This is the best tree ever!" In those days, each of us received one present, which we found under the tree. We were not allowed to pick it up, touch it, or shake it, for fear that we would find out what the contents were and ruin the surprise on Christmas Day. Sometimes our parents would fool us, and put fake boxes under the tree, and hide the real presents in a closet or down in the basement somewhere. The best part of Christmas was getting together with relatives, to share with each other what ever we had. I remember extending our dining room table to squeeze in twenty or more people. Our relatives would arrive on Christmas Eve and stay overnight. It would be a fun time for us kids as we got to sleep on the plush carpet. A pillow and a blanket completed our bedding. The grown-ups would sleep in our beds. Of course we got very little sleep. Spending a night with cousins seldom seen leads to conversations carried on long into the night. For the next holiday, the procedure would be reversed, and we would spend the night at our cousins' house, getting to sleep on their floor.

I also remember the many New Year's Eves we celebrated in Brooklyn. At the stroke of midnight, practically all the families on the block would go out into the street, regardless of the cold. With pots and pans and wooden spoons, we made as much noise as possible. The kids would usually get the covers of the pots and pans, and we would bang them together trying to

The Lady From Hell

make more noise than our neighbors. After about five or ten minutes of this insanity, we would all go back into our houses, half frozen, to a table full of goodies, including all kinds of cakes, pastries, pies, candies, hot coffee or tea, and hot chocolate.

As a teenager, I noticed how much Brooklyn was changing. More and more people were moving in, and the empty lots were being replaced by new homes. Cars and trucks were replacing the old horse-drawn wagons, and I anticipated there would be some big changes in the very near future.

These were some of the beautiful memories I would be leaving behind when I went into the service. I also left behind a beautiful and loving family, and I would lose them for over three long years. There would be times during the war when I thought I had lost them forever.

2

THE BULLETIN

I remember December 7, 1941, as if it were yesterday. It was a clear, cold Sunday in Brooklyn, and I was listening to the New York Giants/Brooklyn Dodgers football game. There was no television in those days. The game was being broadcast on the radio. Professional football was in its infancy, and Brooklyn had its own professional team. I don't recall the score, but, as was the case with most intercity rivalries, the game was very exciting. Needless to say, I was quite annoyed when they interrupted the game to bring us this important "bulletin." The bulletin said that, at 0900 hours that morning, the Royal Japanese Navy and Air Force had attacked Pearl Harbor. The bulletin continued on to say that the attack wreaked much havoc and inflicted tremendous damage to the unsuspecting

Americans who were based at Pearl Harbor. The announcer tried, as best he could, not to panic the people, but as the news kept filtering in, it became quite clear that the attack had caused complete devastation. Many lives were lost. Henderson Airport was completely destroyed. Fires were raging out of control all over the island. Our Air Force had been destroyed on the ground, before it ever had a chance to get into the air. And, to make matters worse, half of our Navy lay under water. Japan's Navy and Air Force had indeed done a job on us. Pearl Harbor lay in ruins, and the American people were in complete shock. How ironic that, at the time of the attack on Pearl Harbor, there were two Japanese envoys in Washington talking peace with our government. I did not realize what a tremendous impact that bulletin would have on my life, and on the lives of millions of families throughout the world.

The following day, President Franklin Delano Roosevelt declared war on Japan,

The Lady From Hell

Germany, and Italy. The United States was now totally involved in World War II.

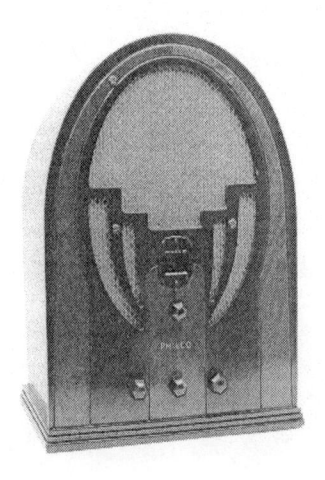

Many American families heard the devastating news of Pearl Harbor while listening to radios such as this Philco. Antique radio image used with permission from Phil's Old Radios website, http://antiqueradio.org/index.html, copyright © 1995-2000, Philip I. Nelson, all rights reserved.

I may be getting a little ahead of my story, but I must tell you a little bit about what a great man President Roosevelt was, and what a great leader he turned out to be. He had many physical problems and, among other things, he was paralyzed from the waist down as a result of polio. He was confined to a wheelchair. He was truly a wonderful person and during those early years of the war, he led our country through many bleak and dismal times. It must be remembered, that in the beginning following the declaration of war, the United States and its Allies suffered tremendous losses, both in Europe and in The Pacific. The low point of the war was the Death March our soldiers had to take, after our surrender of the Philippine Islands to the Japanese Army. The heat during this march was unforgiving, and the soldiers marched for days on end, with no food or water. The march took is toll. Many American Soldiers died on this brutal march, and those who survived lived to tell of the horrors and the brutality of the Japanese Army. So it fell to President Roosevelt to give the sad news to the American People. He acknowledged our defeats and even suggested they would get worse before they got better. He thanked the American People for all their suffering and sacrifices they were making.

The Lady From Hell

He reminded us that our nation was getting stronger and stronger with each passing day, and soon the odds would be in our favor. In the end, he promised victory would be ours. He was truly an inspiration to the entire nation, and everyone looked forward to his weekly "Fireside Chats." President Roosevelt died in the spring of 1945, and the entire world mourned his passing. I thought to myself how sad it was that this great American would not be around to enjoy the surrender of the Axis powers and taste the fruits of victory, a victory in which he was so instrumental. The war was nearing an end, and it was only a matter of time. He had come so close, with the war ending only months after his death.

I was in Russia at the time of his death, and I was quite surprised how many Russian people expressed their sorrow. "Rest in peace, President Roosevelt" and "Thank you" were sentiments widely expressed.

3

GRADUATION

I was a seventeen year old high school senior attending New Utrecht High School in Brooklyn when war was declared. I was scheduled to graduate in June of 1942. I was not a very good student, sometimes just barely managing to pass. It was not that I was stupid or lazy; I just preferred playing sports over studying. There were many times I would cut classes to play ball. It was rumored around the school at that time, that because of the war, everyone in the senior class would graduate, even those with failing grades. Some of the students thought that if they flunked out, it would keep them out of the military service for another year. Unfortunately, this was a fallacy and proved not to be the case. Regardless of one's grades or graduation status, when we turned eighteen years of age, we knew

Frank J. Condreras

we would be hearing very soon from Uncle Sam. Despite all the rumors, I knew of no one who did not graduate that year. The teachers worked above and beyond, especially with the marginal students.

With a war looming overhead, graduation was not the usual joyous occasion for my generation.

So it came to pass that some two thousand students graduated New Utrecht High School in June of 1942. Because of the tremendous number of students, our exercises had to be held in Prospect Park.

The Lady From Hell

We were all hoping it would not rain, and indeed it turned out to be a beautiful warm and sunny day. If only the mood matched the weather. This joyous occasion turned somber when one of the speakers of our high school gave his speech.

He began on a positive note by commending us and congratulating us, but his thoughts then turned to the war. He predicted that within six months or so, most of us young men would be drafted into the service. He verbalized what lay heavy on our minds; that many of us would never return. Although foremost in our minds, it was in poor taste to mention this at what was to be a celebration ceremony. After the exercises, I left with my parents, as most of the graduates did. There was not a dry eye in Prospect Park that day. My parents had planned a little party for me, in honor of my graduation. Most of my close relatives were there, including some of my friends. We drank and we ate, and we were having a good time, yet I could not help but notice the worried looks on the faces of some of the parents, including mine. We were all very careful to avoid the subject of the war.

Speaking of the war, it was beginning to have an effect on the American way of life. Aside from families losing their loved ones to the military service, many items were now getting harder to find. Items such as sugar, meats, and gasoline were being rationed. The dance halls, nightclubs, and movie houses were closing in record numbers. Even our prom was cancelled. I do not think anybody cared one way or the other. I know I didn't.

4

THE INDUCTION

It was June of 1942. I had just graduated high school, and college was out of the question. The war had escalated, affecting every family one way or another. We were losing the war very badly, or as one newspaper put it, "We were getting our butts kicked." The war in the Pacific had become a disaster. Many of the Pacific Islands were now under Japanese control. The Philippine Islands and the Island of Corregador also fell, chasing General McArthur and his staff to Australia. It was at this time that General McArthur promised the Philippine people that he would return. In Europe, the situation was just as bad. Many countries surrendered to the German onslaught. England was being bombed day and night, and bracing itself for an invasion. German armies were marching towards the Russian capital of Moscow.

In the meantime, our nation was biding its time, getting bigger and stronger every day. Army camps were springing up all over the nation. From all over the United States, hundreds of thousands, indeed millions of men were being inducted into the military service. War plants and defense factories were going full force. I found myself working in one of these defense plants. It was located in Long Island City. The pay was good and you worked as many hours as you liked. There was time and a half and double time pay for the asking. I would work twelve hours a day, six days a week. The plant was open twenty-four hours a day, seven days a week. It never closed.

The defense plant for which I was working made stretchers for our Army, Navy, Air Force, and all our allies. I don't know the exact number of stretchers we made, but every week we would make more stretchers than the previous week. Since these stretchers were used to carry the wounded in the war, I figured they must have been expecting an awful lot of casualties. Be that as it may, I was making more money than I ever dreamed possible. But all good things come to an end. Early in 1943, I received notification from the war department that I was to report to Whitehall Street, in New York City, to take my physical examination.

    I could not believe my eyes when I came out of the subway station. The lines at the Whitehall Street Building stretched around the building and down several blocks. I would estimate there were several thousand of us waiting to get in. To make matters worse, it was raining and cold. Once I got into the building, there was mass confusion. There were not enough doctors to handle the huge number of people. I finally took a very abbreviated physical, and needless to say, I passed, as most everyone did. It was my impression at the time that, if your body was warm and you could move your arms and legs, you would pass.

Frank J. Condreras

'Greetings' from President Roosevelt, inviting me to join the military.

    I was classified as "1A," which simply meant that in a month or so, I would be receiving greetings from "Uncle Sam." I kept working because, as I stated previously, the pay was good and it helped my family financially. About five or six weeks later, I

The Lady From Hell

received those greetings from "Uncle Sam" telling me that I was to report to Grand Central Station. It was three days before Easter when this news came. I could not understand why the Army could not have waited three more days so that I could spend Easter at home with my family. Maybe it was for the best, since it would not be a very happy occasion. I was eighteen years old. I was not old enough to drink at a bar, but I was old enough to kill.

So, on that Holy Thursday, I reported to Grand Central Station. I had taken the subway with a friend and my cousin, who lived with us. I did not want my parents to come. I was afraid there would be a scene, and I did not want to see my mother crying any more than she already had. How hard it must have been for a mother and father to send their eighteen-year-old son to a war. How harder yet for the parents who sent two or three sons? In the past, when an eighteen-year-old son or daughter said goodbye to their parents, they were probably going to some college away from home. They would be back, eventually. Unfortunately, my generation did not have a choice, and there was no guarantee that we would be returning.

I couldn't help but wonder how many families were being torn apart like this all over the world. With misty eyes, I said goodbye to my cousin and my friend, and joined a large group of future soldiers. The sergeant in charge started calling names, and I was assigned to a train. I took a seat and waited...and waited...and waited some more. After two long hours, the train finally began to move. I would come to find out that, in the Army, I would always be rushing to get on a long line to wait. This was the Army's way. As we pulled out of the station, the sergeant informed us that we were on our way to Fort Dix in New Jersey. My journey had begun. It would be a long journey; one that would last almost three years. It was during these years that a lifetime of memories was created, memories that will remain with me forever.

5

FORT DIX

It took about four hours to get to Fort Dix, a trip that should have taken half that time. It was less than a luxurious ride that made many stops along the way. It was about eight o'clock in the evening when the army trucks met us at the train station to take us to the mess hall. We were all quite hungry, as no one had eaten since breakfast. I was looking forward to my first meal in the army. Unfortunately it consisted of a half-frozen bologna sandwich on two stale pieces of bread, a container of milk, and a donut. A very irate mess sergeant further informed us that we were lucky to get anything at all, since the mess hall had to be reopened just to accommodate us. After this tremendous meal, the sergeant had us form a line outside the mess hall. We walked about a mile in the rain to a warehouse where we were issued bedding and blankets and assigned to a barracks. I spent a miserable first night in the army. I was cold, wet, and hungry, and I could not sleep on that narrow army cot. The events of the day kept running through my head. First there was the motor pool; the drivers had arrived at the train station at six o'clock to pick us up. We did not arrive until eight o'clock, so they were waiting for over two hours. Then there was the mess sergeant and his crew who had to reopen the mess hall. Lastly there was the quarter master group who issued us our bedding, and they were also annoyed because we were so late. I had been in Fort Dix a little over an hour and already there were three outfits angry with our group. It was not until about four o'clock in the morning that I finally got to sleep. One hour later, the bugle sounded and everybody got up.

We were told by the sergeant in charge that we would be having breakfast at seven. Therefore we had two hours to shave, shower, make up our bunks and get ready. We were still wearing our civilian clothing when we marched into the mess hall. I was starving, as were most of us. I enjoyed breakfast tremendously. They had powdered scrambled eggs, sausage, home fried potatoes, toast, cereals, and all sorts of donuts. I went up for seconds and, for the first time in the last several days, I was feeling good. The rest of the day was spent on long lines, receiving clothes such as underwear, shoes, socks, shirts, pants, jacket, overcoats, etc. Later that afternoon we were taken to a movie house to watch a film about sexually transmitted diseases. I fell asleep during the movie, as did most of the others. It was dark and warm inside, and the seats were so comfortable. I was so tired I just dozed off.

On the second day, I received several vaccinations. I was also given a book with the information of what injections I had received, and the dates they were given. This book stayed with me wherever I went throughout my army career. I also received another physical exam. I guess the army did not believe the Whitehall Street doctors from New York City.

On Easter Sunday, I was assigned "KP" in the officers' mess hall. I was in the army three days and I was already assigned KP. I was told I was lucky because the food in the officers' mess was the best, especially on holidays, and that I could eat all I wanted. It was true. We had ham, turkey, steaks, and everything from soup to nuts. Between breakfast, lunch and dinner, I ate like a king. The first job I was assigned to during KP was peeling potatoes. As a young boy, I had read about KP for the GI's in World War I. The pictures usually depicted several pathetic-looking soldiers sitting in front of a huge pile of potatoes. Since potatoes were a staple food at almost every meal in the armed forces, these poor soldiers could be peeling potatoes for the rest of their lives. This is what I had envisioned when I received my potato assignment. I did not realize how modern our army had become. Now, instead of peeling potatoes by hand, a bushel of potatoes was put into a huge

The Lady From Hell

machine, similar to a clothes dryer. These machines had very rough sandpaper which lined the inside walls, and as the machine spun around, the skin would scrape off the potatoes. When the cycle was completed, the potatoes were peeled. We would then "eye" the deep cuts that the machine might have missed. You could peel a large amount of potatoes in a very short time. There was, however, a lot of waste, as the potatoes would come out much smaller than they went in. But with so many mouths to feed, time was more important. All in all, KP in the officers' mess hall was not that bad. The only drawback was that the day started at four o'clock in the morning and ended at eight o'clock in the evening. No matter how you added, subtracted, multiplied, or divided, sixteen hours made for a very long day.

I missed my family that Easter Sunday. It was the first holiday I had ever been away and I kept thinking of them all day long. Three days away from home felt like a year. Despite the good food, I was depressed all day. I did get to phone them to wish them all a happy Easter. I felt better after that, even though my sister and mother cried on the phone.

After that KP, my duties varied. I was assigned minor jobs such as typing at headquarters, cleaning areas of cigarette butts, and so on. One day, I even got to drive an army jeep. I was to go to the train station, pick up the mail, and bring it back to headquarters. The mail was for the men who were based at Fort Dix. As I was driving back with the mail, I realized how huge Fort Dix was. It just went on for miles and miles. Barracks were being built in massive numbers.

About a week after our arrival, I was informed, along with several hundred others, to pack my gear because we were shipping out. We were leaving to start our basic training and everything was a secret. No one knew where we were headed. Most of us reasoned that since we were issued only winter clothing, we would be heading

The Lady From Hell

some place north for our basic training. It sounded logical, but then again, there is nothing logical about the army. The next day we boarded the train and left Fort Dix for an unknown destination.

Little did I realize that, in about three years, I would be returning to this same Fort Dix, however the circumstances this time would be quite different.

6

BASIC TRAINING

Although we were on the train since 0900 hours, we did not leave Fort Dix until about noon. We still did not know where we were going. The train proceeded through Delaware, Washington D.C., Virginia, the Carolinas, Georgia, and then Florida. One thing was certain; we were not headed north. We finally ended up in Miami. The trip had taken over two days. We slept very uncomfortably in our hard seats. The lurching, stopping, breaking, and squeaking made it very difficult to sleep for any length of time. The train had made several stops along the way to allow us to exercise. They also stopped for food and water to accommodate the many soldiers on board. It also gave the cars on the train a good airing out. There were no shower facilities on the train. We barely had enough water to wash our hands and face before each meal. To make matters worse, the train was very warm and stuffy. Not only were we overcrowded, we were all wearing winter clothing, including long johns. The odor was overwhelming. So it was with great relief that we left the train to board the army trucks that would be taking us to Miami Beach, our home for the next four or five months. I was in awe. I had never been further south than Coney Island, and here I was in Miami. Brooklyn seemed so far away now.

The trucks rolled into Miami Beach, and I was assigned a room at the Caribbean Hotel. There were many beautiful hotels along Collins Avenue in Miami Beach, but none as beautiful as the Caribbean Hotel. I considered myself quite lucky, and my luck kept getting better. My room was a beauty as well. It was very spacious and plush, with a very large bathroom, including closed shower facilities. The room was located on the corner of the building. One set of windows faced the ocean, and the other set faced an Olympic-sized swimming pool.

The Lady From Hell

I envisioned a beautiful breeze that would be all ours to enjoy during the hot summer months of our training period. I shared this room with three other soldiers. Our only responsibility was to keep the room clean and neat at all times. The four of us took turns making sure that the room was indeed clean and neat at all times. There was no way we wanted to lose this beautiful room, and since we passed all the frequent surprise inspections, we must have been doing a good job.

Basic training, we were told, would last three months, after which we would be sent to a place called "Tent City" for an additional month of basic training. The sergeant informed us of this shortly after being assigned our room. Sergeant Krupp was to be our drill instructor for the period it took us to complete our basic training. He was a man about thirty years of age and in fantastic physical shape. He came from the midwestern part of the United States. He informed us, in no uncertain terms and with much vulgarity, that he was "GOD," and that we were to follow his orders at all times, whether we liked them or not. He was going to work our butts off, and we were going to learn to hate him. The more we hated him, the better he would like it. His message was loud and clear. We were all very impressed and intimidated.

This is me with a buddy in front of the Caribbean Hotel. We were in Basic Training at the time.

The Lady From Hell

Our group consisted of about eighty green (novice) and scared soldiers, and it was Sergeant Krupp's duty to ensure that by the end of basic training we became competent soldiers. I never got in trouble with the sergeant. I stayed away from him as much as possible, and I obeyed all his orders to the letter. I kept a very low profile with him, but I felt that, underneath all his toughness, he was a pretty nice person. I also sensed that he was a lonely man who missed his home and loved ones. That was something that we all had in common. Despite being mean and tough, he possessed all the qualities of being a decent human being.

After this, our basic training started in earnest. The first few days were not very exciting. I was given another physical, more vaccinations, and a dental exam. This was my third physical within the last month. We would now be going to all our functions in formation. Sergeant Krupp would now be marching at our side at all times. He stuck to us like glue. "Hup-Hup-Hip-Ho, get in step, Hup-Hup-Hip-Ho, get in step, Hip-Ho." Many times during the day he'd pull someone out of formation to make sure he knew his left from his right. Basic training itself was a repetition of events, day after day, Monday through Friday. Our training site was the parade grounds, which was located over two miles from our hotel. We would march there in the mornings, come back for lunch, and then march back to the parade grounds. It was eight daily miles of marching just to get to the training site. With temperatures constantly over 90 degrees, it was definitely not a fun time. When we got there, our training would begin in earnest. First, calisthenics including push-ups and sit-ups, then the dreaded obstacle course would follow, and finally, the drill and dress marching. Also, there would be gas mask drills and lectures on the different types of guns which we would encounter during the course of the war. The march to the parade grounds in the morning was not bad, but returning in the late afternoon was a killer. We were dirty, tired, and sweaty,

The Lady From Hell

and if we goofed in any part of our training, Sergeant Krupp would have us double-time back to the hotel. We goofed quite often, so we did a lot of running. I felt sorry for the older soldiers in our platoon; the over-thirty group. They had problems keeping up with the younger soldiers. Some of them were so exhausted that, upon returning from the day's training, they would flop down on their bunks, and not wake up until five o'clock reveille the next morning. Personally, as tired as I was, I never missed any meals. Our days would always begin at 0500 hours for the roll call outside the hotel. Then we'd go back to our rooms, make up our bunks, shower, shave, and then head off to the mess hall for breakfast. After this we would head out to the parade grounds for the start of another day. Everything we did was in formation, no matter where we went or what we did; with the sergeant right at our side every step of the way.

   The only thing that would provide relief from this routine was the one day a week we would be assigned KP duty, and the one day the following week we would be assigned guard duty. Both assignments required sixteen hours of your time. Guard duty entailed two hours on duty and two hours off, and it consisted of patrolling a mile-long stretch of beach. I did not mind beach patrol during daylight hours, but at night it was a very boring and lonely job. There were rumors going around that German submarines were landing German spies along the Miami Beach coastline. This made guard duty at night even more frightening. Many times guards called for the sergeant of the guards during the night, because they thought they saw something coming out of the water or land on the beach. The shadows at night, and the noise made by the waves as they broke on the shore, made you think you were seeing things that were not there. It was quite an eerie feeling. I was very happy when my guard duty assignment was over. There is not much to say about KP. You ate well, but you worked very hard for sixteen hours. Needless to say, I was also very happy when this assignment was over. As I stated previously, basic training was a repetitive routine, with these two exceptions.

On Saturdays, we had parade day. We would parade in front of our commanding General and the other visiting dignitaries. I hated these Saturday parades with a passion. Several thousand soldiers from all over Miami Beach participated, and it took hours before we were fully assembled and ready to march. During the summer months the heat was unrelenting, always over ninety degrees. Since we marched in full gear, the sun would beat down on our steel helmets. The metal got so hot that, at times, you felt like your brain was frying and your head was on fire. There were many ambulances lined up along the parade route to pick up the soldiers who had fallen or passed out completely from heat exhaustion. We were told not to stop to pick these fallen soldiers up. We were to step over them and continue marching. The attendants from the ambulances would assist the fallen soldiers and place them on stretchers. I immediately recognized the stretchers as the same ones I was making in the defense plant where I worked before Uncle Sam sent me his greetings. After we passed the reviewing stand, we headed "home" to our rooms at the hotel. As we marched further from the parade grounds, we could still hear the band playing songs such as "Yankee Doodle Dandy," "The Yanks Are Coming Over There," or "Give My Regards To Broadway." Because of the length of the parade, these songs were repeated many times.

Sunday was our day off. It was a time to catch up on writing letters, washing your clothes, and sleeping late. If any time was left, we could use the beach or the pool, both of which were located three floors below us. Even the P.X. was located in our building on the ground floor, and it was open to enlisted men on Saturdays and Sundays. Here you could eat, drink and relax. The P.X. was a fun place, and the beer was always cold. Needless to say,

The Lady From Hell

Sundays were, by far, the best days of the week.

Our basic training was nearing its completion. It was over three months since we started, and you could tell that Sergeant Krupp was very pleased with our progress and proud of himself for this accomplishment. He did not yell anymore, as he had no reason to. Our formations were now quickly formed and we lined up perfectly each and every time. When we marched, we had a bounce to our step. The songs we sang while marching were clear and loud. Everybody in Miami Beach knew it was Sergeant Krupp's outfit marching down Collins Avenue. At the end of basic training, I was in the best shape of my life. I weighed only 135 pounds, but every ounce of it was lean, and I felt good. I was even enjoying the dreaded obstacle course. During the last week of basic training, Sergeant Krupp informed us that beginning next week we would be leaving Miami Beach for "Tent City." We would spend three to four weeks in "Tent

City," depending on our progress, and that would conclude our basic training. We would then return to Miami Beach to await our next assignment.

"Tent City" was a swamp located some twenty miles from Miami Beach. The first time I saw it, I hated it. It consisted of nothing but tents, rows and rows of tents, the biggest of which was the mess hall. We marched these twenty miles in full gear, with practically everything we owned on our backs. It was a long and tiring march, and we arrived quite late. We were all very hungry, as we had not eaten since breakfast. Everyone was grateful that the mess hall had remained open for us, and, I must say, everyone ate with gusto. After our dinner we were assigned our tents. There were six of us to a tent. "Tent City" had no plumbing facilities at all, so all the food and water had to be trucked in. To make matters worse, on each row of tents there hung a huge canvas bag full of water with a spigot on the bottom. This was our drinking water. Since it hung all day long

The Lady From Hell

in the hot sun, the water was very warm, and it was also full of quinine and various other chemicals so that it would be safe to drink. It tasted absolutely horrible; "My kingdom for a cold beer!" I thought. Our bodily functions were performed in freshly dug pits, which were covered with lime from time to time, to keep the odor down and the flies away. It did not work. The smell was terrible, and to make matters worse, there were billions of mosquitoes. The swamp was a breeding ground for them. If you had diarrhea, which many soldiers experienced, you were in big trouble.

Our tents were comfortable enough, except when it rained and everything became a mudslide. Thankfully, the days went by very quickly. We had classes on all types of weapons, pistols, rifles, and sub-machine guns. We had target practice using all the different weapons. One day we were on the pistol range, another day on the rifle range, another on the machine gun range. We even got involved in skeet shooting, which was a lot of fun. I really enjoyed this phase of training. It was the first time in my life that I ever fired a gun.

It was here that I received my first medal from the army. It was for marksmanship, and I was quite proud of it. Our tour of duty in "Tent City" also required some of the "basics" learned in basic training, such as climbing walls, digging foxholes, crawling under barbed wire, and eating "K rations" out of the can. I felt sure, at this point, that I was headed for the infantry. When our tour of duty was finished at "Tent City," we were taken back to our hotel, via army trucks. My room never looked so good, especially the shower. In "Tent City" the water was rationed and we were allowed to shower two times a week. This shower consisted of a quick splash of water to soap yourself, then another quick splash of water to rinse yourself off. That was their idea of a shower. It was not mine, nor was it my fellow soldiers'. Needless to say, the shower in our room was busy that day. If you pardon the expression, we were now considered seasoned soldiers. We

The Lady From Hell

had completed our basic training and, as a reward, I received my first stripe. I was now Private First Class, Frank J. Condreras.

The next two weeks were a waiting game. We had no duties to perform, no marching or drilling, no guard duty or KP. We just waited around. On occasion, we would take different types of tests such as IQ tests, aptitude tests, mechanical tests, and so on. I was so bored that I would run the obstacle course several times a day. Some of my buddies thought I was nuts. I had not seen Sergeant Krupp since our return from "Tent City," until one day when I saw him in front of a new group of soldiers. He was giving them the same speech he had given my group more than four months ago. I felt sorry for these green soldiers, because I knew what lay ahead for them. At least it was September now, and they would have cooler weather than we did.

Several days later I received my orders to ship out, and once again everything became very secretive. No one knew where we were going. I was having mixed emotions. Although I was happy I had completed basic training, I was sad to be leaving Miami Beach and the many friends I had made. I would come to find out that, throughout my army career, this would happen many times. I saw Sergeant Krupp for the last time that day. As I left, he was headed out to the parade grounds with his new group of soldiers, his voice loud and clear. The army had given him a job to do, and he was doing it to the best of his ability. God speed, Sergeant Krupp, and good luck!

We boarded the trucks that took us to the train station and got on the train immediately. I was pleasantly surprised, because the train was not only clean, it had beautifully cushioned seats that tilted back to a comfortable resting position. The car was also air-conditioned. The conditions were certainly a far cry from the cattle cars that had brought us to basic training so many months ago. The train pulled out of Miami both smoothly and in a timely manner. I was on my way...to some place, and basic training was now a part of the past.

I could dedicate this entire book to basic training and the many associated experiences, but there are a few things that bear significance for me, personally. It was a known fact, that if you wanted to get out of KP and guard duty, you could volunteer for other activities that were available. So I joined the boxing team. I fought three times, winning the first two fights and losing the third one. The morning after my last fight, I woke up to an eye that was swollen shut, a puffed up face, and lots of cuts and bruises. My career as a fighter ended very abruptly that morning when I quit the boxing team.

Frank J. Condreras

I had a very short boxing career while in Florida for Basic Training. (I'm the one still standing!)

Then there were the baseball throwing contests, where we would gather on the beach to see who could throw a baseball the farthest. We would take bets on the

The Lady From Hell

winners. Most of the bets were for five dollars. I knew from my ball-playing days in Brooklyn, that God had blessed me with a good arm and I could throw a baseball a long way. This contest was made for me. I threw against guys much bigger than myself and often had no trouble winning. Some of my buddies arranged contests with soldiers from other platoons. I always did well. Everyone was amazed that this skinny kid from Brooklyn could throw a ball so far. Most of the guys against whom I competed were much bigger than me, but they just did not know how to throw a baseball. My buddies and I usually made ourselves a few dollars.

Finally, there was the time when we were returning from a parade one Saturday afternoon. We were covered with dirt and grime. The parade ground had been a dust bowl. Perspiration had penetrated our uniforms, and we were soaked in our own sweat. Meanwhile, as we kept marching, Sergeant Krupp kept "Hup-hupping" all the way back to the hotel. However, this time, instead of halting our formation in front of the hotel and dismissing us, he kept us marching right past the hotel, onto the beach, and into the ocean. I must say that the water felt so good, and Sergeant Krupp marched right along with us into the ocean. I could still hear him giving cadence when a wave hit him and he went under.

Many experiences similar to these happened day after day, and the stories are numerous. Personally, I enjoyed basic training. I did everything asked of me, and I felt I did it well. It was an experience that will stay with me the rest of my life.

The Lady From Hell

This picture was taken just after the completion of Basic Training.

AIRPLANE MECHANIC SCHOOL

As our train moved up the west coast of Florida, rumors started spreading regarding our destination, which could be anywhere from Maine to California, but no one knew for sure. When our train reached Tallahassee, Florida, we turned towards the west. We passed through Alabama, Mississippi, Louisiana, and then into Texas. Several times a day, our train would pull over on some sidetracks, so that we could do some exercises. I looked forward to these exercises. Just getting off the train and stretching your legs made you feel good. At several of these stops, the American Red Cross met us with fresh donuts and coffee. I could not thank these wonderful people from the American Red Cross enough. They were all volunteers who took time out of their lives to make life for the servicemen nicer. During the course of the war, I would be even more grateful to them. I was also becoming a pretty good poker player. With so much time available, practically everyone played poker; win or lose, it made time go by quickly.

The train ride lasted four days, and we finally ended up in Amarillo. It was a city in the "Pan Handle" part of Texas. The army trucks were there waiting to take us to camp. There was also a large army band to welcome us. I remember them playing "The Eyes of Texas Are Upon You" and "The Yellow Rose of Texas." When the trucks rolled into camp we were met by a Captain, whose name I do not remember. He welcomed us to the Amarillo Air Force Base. He informed us that the base was constructed very hastily when the war broke out. In fact, workers were still building new barracks and laying wooden planks over the dirt sidewalks. When we arrived, we were told we would be attending an airplane mechanic school, which would last three months. The last phase of school would be spent in the bivouac area. In this area

The Lady From Hell

combat conditions would be simulated to the best extent possible. I was thinking that I might have lucked out, since airplane mechanics usually operated long distances from the battlefronts.

Anyway, the Captain went on to inform us that our time would be pretty much our own, almost, as we were basically college students. Calisthenics would be every morning at 0900 hours, and the rest of the day would be spent in classes that were located in the two hangars near the runways. The mess hall hours were 0600 to 0800 hours for breakfast, 1100 to 1300 hours for lunch, and 1700 to 1900 hours for dinner. Roll call would be at 0700 hours. That in itself was a blessing, as I was under the impression that all army bases started roll call at 0500 hours. Another blessing for us was that we were allowed to go to the mess hall anytime we wanted, within these time frames. We no longer had to go in formation and wait on long lines to get in. If we wanted to skip a meal, that was

Frank J. Condreras

strictly up to us. The Captain could care less.

When the Captain finished his "Welcome Aboard" speech, we were assigned to barracks, each of which housed thirty of us, fifteen on each side of the room. The house sergeant in charge had his own enclosed room. His job was to make sure that the barracks were kept neat and clean at all times. He would wake us up at 0700 hours for roll call, and make sure we were all in at night. This was his house, and you obeyed his rules, or you would have to perform extra duties.

This was our graduation picture taken after completing Airplane Mechanic School.

The Lady From Hell

Several days after we arrived in Amarillo, we started our airplane mechanics training. It was pretty much what the Captain had said it would be. I felt like a student going to school, and I enjoyed it tremendously. The classrooms were comfortable and clean, and airplane mechanics was a subject I liked. It was also knowledge that might be useful after the war. Our faculty consisted of some army personnel, but mostly civilians, and I was very impressed as to how well-informed these people were. I was even more impressed when I found out that several of these instructors, both men and women, had pilot's licenses. The airplanes on which we worked were AT-10's, single-engine airplanes used mainly for naval aviation training. We removed and replaced different parts of this airplane. In fact, at the end of our training, we were able to remove and replace the entire engine within a couple of hours. We also made repairs to the framework. We got to start the engines, taxi the plane, and use the many tools available to us. We pulled inspections on various parts of the aircraft. It was a fun time.

Saturdays and Sundays were our days off, and we got to do what ever we wanted. The barrack sergeant had advised us that after one month we would be allowed weekend passes to Amarillo, and I was looking forward to that. Our field contained a beautiful P.X., which sold frankfurters, hamburgers, and all kinds of shakes, or beer, if you preferred. The atmosphere was a little bit different than that of the mess hall. There was also a movie house and bowling alley available to us on the field. Saturdays and Sundays were good "catch-up" days. The first month of our training went by very fast and, before I knew it, I was receiving my first pass. I was going to be a civilian for two days. I could hardly wait to see the town of Amarillo.

Army trucks were our sole transportation in and out of town. They would leave the base and return periodically.

The Lady From Hell

The last truck back to base would leave town at 2200 hours each night. If you missed that one, you were stuck overnight. Amarillo was a city suffering from the war, just like most other cities in the United States. The civilian people treated us well, and with respect. Many of them had loved ones in the service, possibly in combat areas, so they certainly had reason to be concerned. I found the Texans to be very proud people, and very hospitable, with hearts as big as their state. Amarillo had several movie houses, some bowling alleys, some very good bars, but most of all, it had very good restaurants. Even until today, I have never been to a restaurant that served the quality steaks they served in Amarillo. The steaks were as big as the large platters on which they were served, smothered with mushrooms and onions. A large baked potato (everything in Texas is large), and a huge salad, completed the feast. On my first visit, my buddies and I tried to get a room at several hotels, to stay overnight, but there were no vacancies, so we caught the last army truck back to base. During the rest of my stay in Amarillo, I went to town several times to eat those delicious steaks. This was, indeed, cattle country. I made a promise to myself that, someday, if I survived the war, I would come back to visit Amarillo.

Meanwhile, I was enjoying my life on the base. School was a snap, and we had lots of time on our hands. Even the meals in the mess hall were good. Many mornings they would serve pancakes and/or waffles, with eggs and home fries. On Saturdays and Sundays, we had a ball, a football, that is. It was the fall season, and the weather was turning cold. It was tailor-made for football. Each barrack had their own team, and the games became quite competitive. Except for bragging rights, it did not matter which team won or lost, since after each game we would all end up in the P.X. drinking beer, joking, laughing, and discussing which team was luckier. All week long, I would be looking forward to the weekends. I enjoyed playing so

The Lady From Hell

much. Army life was not bad at all, if only there was no war going on. Unfortunately, as always, the good times ended quickly. Almost three months had passed, and we were finished with the ground school part of our training.

The following week, we were to be sent to the bivouac area, to simulate working under combat conditions. There were several reasons I hated this week. Firstly, we were out in the field during Thanksgiving week. Secondly, the weather had really turned cold. I certainly was not looking forward to sleeping on the cold ground in sleeping bags. There would be many times when I would think of those warm barracks, clean sheets, and hot showers. There was no mess hall at the bivouac, which was another reason for disliking this area. In fact, there were no buildings at all, with the exception of one tent, which was for officers only, and also served to keep our records safe from inclement weather.

Our food was trucked in from the base. The chefs tried their best to keep it as hot as possible, but several minutes after it was served to you, it would already have gotten cold. The stews they served had to be eaten very quickly, or the grease would start to form on the edge of your tray before you finished. Even the wrenches and other tools, with which we worked, would freeze in our hands. The conditions were horrible. One night, we went to sleep in our sleeping bags, and woke up with several inches of snow covering us. This was certainly not one of my better periods in the army. Some very sick soldiers were sent back to the base. Some had the flu, some had pneumonia, and several were sent back with frostbite. Maybe they were luckier than those of us who stayed healthy. On Thanksgiving Day, we saw four or five army trucks roll into the bivouac area to take us to the base mess hall for Thanksgiving dinner. No one had expected this, and we were in total shock, but very grateful we had not been forgotten. I went up for seconds and thirds. The meal was delicious, everything from soup to nuts. I was never so full in all my life. After

The Lady From Hell

dinner, we were taken back to the bivouac area. Somehow, with a full stomach, it did not seem so cold.

Before we knew it, our training was completed, and we were back in base camp. Upon the completion of my training in Amarillo, Texas, I received my second stripe. I was now Corporal, Frank J. Condreras. I was now waiting for my next assignment. Two weeks passed before I was told to pack my bags, because I would be shipping out in the morning. Many of my buddies had already shipped out, and the barracks were practically empty. It was a very lonely time for me. All the friends I made, and played football with, were all gone. The Christmas holidays were approaching, and I felt very much alone. I had mixed feelings when my orders came, and I was taken to the train that would be taking me somewhere for my next assignment. Once again, everything was very secretive. The group with whom I was shipping out was small. There were only about fifty of us. It was also a very young group, soldiers my own age. The train was a civilian train, and many of these civilians were traveling to California. One of the cars on the train was empty, reserved for us soldiers. I thought to myself, which I was doing a lot of lately, that if this train was headed for California, we were bound, in some capacity, to be headed for the Pacific operation. It sounded logical. Right? Wrong! The train stopped in the middle of the desert, in a place called Kingman, Arizona. So much for logic!

The Lady From Hell

United States Army

Army Air Forces Technical School

Be it known that

PRIVATE FIRST CLASS FRANK J. CONDRERAS, ASN 32889656

has satisfactorily completed the course for

Airplane Mechanics

as prescribed by the Commanding General Army Air Forces Technical Training Command and Given at

Amarillo Army Air Field
Amarillo, Texas

In testimony whereof and by virtue of vested authority I do confer upon him this

DIPLOMA

Given on this SEVENTEENTH day of JANUARY in the year of our Lord, one thousand nine hundred and forty-four.

Colonel, Air Corps
COMMANDING
AIR FORCES TECHNICAL SCHOOL

This was the diploma we received after graduation from Airplane Mechanic School.

8

AERIAL GUNNERY SCHOOL

We arrived in Kingman, Arizona, early in the morning. Before the war, with possibly the exception of New York City, I knew very little about the United States. Since being in the army, I was receiving a first-hand education regarding many of our states. I was seeing things that I had only read about in school. I never realized how big and beautiful America was. It was quite evident someone had goofed about our arrival. It may have been the transportation officer, the motor pool, or some clerk who forgot to relay a message about our arrival. We would never know who was to blame, as each would blame the others, and life would go on. Anyway, the buses that were to take us to camp were two hours late, but arrive they did, much to the relief of the officer in charge of us. The camp was quite a distance from where the train had left us, so the ride back to camp was quite lengthy. I could not help but notice how beautiful the desert was, with all the different plants and their beautiful colors. I imagined that the desert sunrises and sunsets must be an amazing sight, and indeed, I would see them many times before leaving Arizona. I could not have imagined just how fantastic and breathtaking they could be.

When we arrived at the base, we were greeted by the company commander. He informed us that during the next three to four months, we would be in aerial gunnery and flight engineer training. We were further informed that the course included both ground and air training. The length of the course depended on the availability of the airplanes.

I now knew what my role was to be for the duration of the war. Upon the completion of this training, I would be a certified flight engineer of the B-17 Flying Fortress. I would be assigned to the European theater of operations. I would be assigned either to the Eighth Air Force

The Lady From Hell

in England, or the Fifteenth Air Force in Italy. It was a very sobering moment, as the odds of completing your missions and coming home were not very good, to say the least. How quickly plans could change. When I graduated mechanic school, I had visions of being a mechanic at some airport far away from any combat. That was no longer possible. I wondered why I was picked for flying duty. Why me? As I looked around at my group, the answer was quite obvious. There were about sixty of us, and we were all about nineteen years of age, give or take a couple of months. I guess the army's theory was that the younger you were, the more gullible you were, and you were not old enough to know any better. So be it. There was no way I could fight it. Whatever would be would eventually be.

The sixty of us were assigned to a two-story barracks. It was the first time since I was in the army that I was in barracks that had more than one floor. The next day we were given a tour of the entire base, including all of the classrooms we would be using. In addition to other skills, we would be learning about the maintenance and operation of the fifty-caliber machine gun. Since the Flying Fortress carried thirteen of these guns, it becomes quite important to know how to cope with any malfunctions that may occur during combat. Upon the completion of this course, most of us would be able to put a fifty-caliber machine gun together in thirty seconds, blind-folded.

After showing us the area for ground classes, we were taken to the airfield where our aerial training would take place. It was the first time I had seen an airplane that had four engines. I was in awe. I was looking at a real B-17 Flying Fortress heavy bomber. It was love at first sight, with its huge tail and wide wings. Even on the ground, she looked so graceful. We were allowed to go into the airplane. I was on cloud nine. It was easy to see why she was called a "Flying Fortress," as there were fifty-caliber machine guns sticking out all over her, thirteen in all.

As training progressed, it became

The Lady From Hell

quite evident that upon the completion of our training we would eventually be headed to the European operations. I tried to put on a brave front, but underneath it all, I was scared, and so were the others with whom I was training. It was no secret that the Eighth Air Force was losing more bombers than our government would admit. Flying over Germany for long periods of time, with no fighter escort, in daylight hours, and against the most powerful air force in the world, did not make the odds of success or longevity for the bomber crews very good. It was a grim picture and, to say the least, it put a damper on our training, even though we progressed through the months without a hitch. Ground classes were a cinch, and flying was like a bonus. Although most of my gunnery training was done in the top turret, I did get to fire the other guns in the plane. But the thing I was most proud of was my work as a flight engineer. I had accumulated about one hundred twenty hours of flight time in school. The months came and passed without much commotion.

Mostly all of us completed our training with flying colors, and the company commander was quite proud, as he congratulated us on doing a fine job. I had accomplished a lot in the three months that I was in Kingman, Arizona. Upon graduation, I received my silver wings, which were to be pinned on the left side of my jacket. I was also a qualified flight engineer and, in addition, was promoted to Sergeant. I liked that. It had a nice ring to it: Sergeant Frank J. Condreras. During my training in Arizona, I also realized that I loved flying. I was in my glory whenever I was in the plane, calling out the airspeed, as we rumbled down the runway, and, as the pilot would pull back on the yoke, feeling the gentle giant lift its nose into the air. What a beautiful, indescribable feeling, breaking out of the overcast sky and into the bright sunlight. I had never gotten sick, no matter how bad the weather was or how much turbulence we experienced. Some of

The Lady From Hell

my buddies were not quite so lucky. Some of them had a fear of flying. I felt sorry for them, as unfortunately, there was no turning back once we were en route, and in the air.

Graduation was not without its reward. I was informed that I was getting a one month leave. It was almost a year since I had seen my family, and I was looking forward to my furlough. I wanted so much to show my family how well I had done in the year I was gone. I was coming home a sergeant, I had silver wings, and I was a qualified flight engineer on the B-17 Flying Fortress. The little boy that left Brooklyn a year ago had become a man.

Traveling during the war could be, at times, a big problem. There was no such thing as air travel. You traveled either by train or by bus. Scheduled arrival and departure times during the war were a joke. The military could "commandeer" a train at any time, for troop movements, and this would cause havoc on the schedules. Fortunately for us, the government had civilian workers, mostly elderly men and women, who worked in different army camps. It was their sole responsibility to get a soldier on leave back and forth, to where he or she had to go. These workers had the authority to have trains and/or buses make unscheduled stops along any route, at anytime, in any place. Many times, you would see a train or bus stop in the middle of nowhere, either to pick up a soldier or let one off.

And so it happened to me. Would you believe that a train, headed from Los Angeles to Chicago, made an unscheduled stop in Kingman, Arizona, just to pick up one soldier – me? To make matters worse for the passengers already on the train, the train picked me up at 0600 hours. The train stopped, a conductor got off, placed his steps on the ground, and, as I stepped up, said "Good morning, sir." It was the first time I had ever been called "Sir." Then again, I never had a train stop just to pick me up. Too bad most of the passengers were asleep. Not many of them realized

The Lady From Hell

what an important person had boarded the train! During the trip, the train made many unscheduled stops, making me realize that I was not so important, after all. With all the stops along the way, it took over four days to get to New York. I did not tell my family what day I was coming home. I wanted to surprise them.

Frank J. Condreras

This was the diploma we received after Aerial Gunnery School.

9

AT LAST, A FURLOUGH

When I arrived in New York, I took a cab from Grand Central Station to Brooklyn. The reception that I received was indescribable. I guess a year away from home is a long time, especially when there is a war going on. I got more hugs and kisses than you can count. Even my dad, who showed very little emotion, hugged me, and I could see tears in his eyes. He was also very proud that I had become a sergeant. My dog, Blackie, never left my side during my entire furlough.

Brooklyn had changed. There were no kids playing ball in the streets. All my friends were in the service, and those who weren't were all working long hours in the defense factories. Even the people of Brooklyn were different. The laughing and joking that I remember was replaced by concern and worry. I'm sure they all had problems relating to the war. So many places had closed. Movie houses, bowling alleys, restaurants, dance clubs, and many small businesses that once thrived were no longer in business. Things were being rationed, causing hardships on the civilian population. It was just not the same old Brooklyn that I used to know.

There wasn't much to do, so I spent my furlough just enjoying the company of my family. I would take my dog Blackie out for walks several times a day, and the time I spent with him in the parks was priceless. It made me realize how much I had missed him. The meals mom cooked were out of this world. Some of the army cooks could have learned a lesson from her. The month went by so quickly that I could not believe it. Oh God, please let this war end soon!

I must share a story with you that took place during my furlough, simply because it's a story worth sharing. My mother had a friend who lived several houses away on our street. They were, indeed, very close friends. This friend, I'll call her "Mrs. M,"

The Lady From Hell

did not speak English very well. She was born and educated in Italy, before coming to the United States. Since she was not an American citizen, my mother thought it would be nice for her to become an American citizen. So my mom filled out the necessary forms and mailed them to the proper authorities. Several weeks later, they received a reply telling them to report to some municipal building in downtown Brooklyn at a certain date and time. Since I was home on furlough at this time, my mother asked me to go with them. She thought that if I wore my uniform, it might influence the judge, and Mrs. M might have a better chance of becoming a citizen. What they did not realize was that you had to pass a test to become a citizen. The questions were quite simple, but because she spoke little English, Mrs. M could not answer them. The judge was very apologetic, and suggested giving Mrs. M the questions to take home to study and coming back the following week for her citizenship test.

    At this point, much to my surprise,

my mother raised her hand and asked to say something on behalf of her friend. As she spoke, the room fell silent. Her story went something like this. "Although Mrs. M has been in this country for many years, she does not speak English very well because she was busy raising five sons and one daughter, and she could not find the time for school." Mom's voice cracked several times, but she continued her story. "Moreover, all five of her sons are in the U.S. military service. One is in the Army, one is in the Marines, and three are in the Navy." My mother was on a roll now. "There are five stars that hang from the windows of her home. There are not many families in the United States that have that distinction. That has to count for something, your honor." My mother had defended her friend well, despite her voice cracking, and I was quite proud of her.

    I could tell that the judge was surprised and, possibly, shaken up. He removed his glasses and wiped his eyes, and as he turned to Mrs. M, he extended his hand

The Lady From Hell

and held out five fingers, and asked, "You have five sons in the service?" With a big smile, Mrs. M answered, "Yes, five sons," and she spoke in English. "Five sons," the judge responded, "and if it weren't for your friend, we would have never known." The judge continued, "I have one son in the service, and I miss him terribly. Mrs. M, I think you are a fantastic lady. You are more of an American citizen than anyone I know, and you certainly don't have to pass any test. Congratulations! As of right now, you are an American citizen!" Emphatically, he stamped several pieces of paper on his desk, giving one to Mrs. M and one to the clerk in the room. With that, the entire room erupted with applause, and it lasted for several minutes.

Mrs. M was still smiling as we left the building. If the truth be known, the real reason Mrs. M had not learned English was because she was a very sick woman. She had been diagnosed with cancer years ago, a cancer for which there was no cure, and that got progressively worse over the years. In fact, the medical professionals involved in her case gave her less than a year to live. You would never know, from the smile on her face, that she had so many problems. Her only wish was that she would live long enough to see all her sons return home from the war. The odds were certainly stacked against her, but Mrs. M would not succumb. She surprised all her doctors and, although she was in constant pain that could only be relieved by morphine injections, she survived the war. Mrs. M passed away several months after her last son had been discharged from the Navy. God had granted her last wish. She died as she had lived, with a smile on her face.

    I enjoyed my furlough tremendously. I was home with my family almost an entire month, but now it was time to get back to the war. It was very difficult to say goodbye, especially when you know that you may not be coming back. It's a horrible feeling, and one that was shared by my family and me. So, after a tearful goodbye, I took a cab from Brooklyn to Grand Central Station. From

The Lady From Hell

there, I would board a train called the "Silver Meteor," which was headed for Miami. I was to report to Miami and check in at the information booth for further orders. The "Silver Meteor" was a civilian train, with plush seats extending outward in a very comfortable position. It felt so good that I closed my eyes as the train left New York. It would be eighteen hours before we would arrive at Miami. That was good. I had a lot to think about.

Frank J. Condreras

This is me on my only furlough. My mom is on the left and Mrs. M is on the right.

10

FLORIDA, THE SECOND TIME

When the "Silver Meteor" arrived in Miami, I was quite surprised how efficient the army was. There were personnel who would look at your orders and tell you what buses to board and where you were to go. I was taken to a place they called Plant Park. To my surprise, there were no barracks. Instead, I was taken to a huge ballpark, and housed together with many others, underneath the stands. There were rows and rows of cots, each with its own footlocker. I was assigned one of these cots and told my stay would be a very short one. It would be here that I would meet the enlisted men of my crew, and I would be with this crew for as long as the war lasted, or until such time as God would permit.

The first crewmember I met was John Wilson, my radio operator. I found him sitting on his cot sipping a coke. I would find out later that John never did drink anything stronger than a soda. He also did not smoke. Everyone else in our crew smoked, as in those days, it was a way of life. I liked John right away. He was from Memphis, Tennessee and had recently been married. You could tell he missed his wife, as he spoke of her often. We were both sergeants when we met, and we became and remained the best of friends throughout the war. Even today, though time and distance have separated us, we remain good friends. On that day, together, we set out to meet the rest of our crew. We knew approximately where to look, and it wasn't long before we began to locate them, one by one.

We found Jim Morgan reading a book, not far from where John and I had met. In combat, Jim would be our right waist gunner and assistant flight engineer. He was from Hollywood, California. He was a soft-spoken, good-looking kid. I thought he should be in Hollywood making movies, instead of fighting a war. He had

The Lady From Hell

enrolled in college, but, unfortunately, the war came along and, like the rest of us, he was drafted into service. He was very lonely and missed his girlfriend, whom he had planned to marry, but again, the war had interfered with his plans. The three of us continued our search for the rest of our crew.

Next we found "Windy" Seward, who was to be our left waist gunner and assistant bombardier. He was with a group of soldiers, laughing and telling jokes. We called him "Windy" because he was always talking. His real name was Richard, but "Windy" seemed to fit him better. He came from the coalmines near Pittsburgh, Pennsylvania. He was from a very large family. At last count, he had twelve brothers and sisters. His family was very poor. Working in the coalmines did not pay very much in those days, so it was necessary for the children to work at very young ages to help support the family. "Windy" was the character of our crew. He had a heart as big as all outdoors; anything he had was yours for the asking, and everybody loved him.

We found our tail gunner sitting on his cot drinking a can of beer. His name was Roy Stemson. He was a big kid from Minnesota. He came from a family of farmers, who grew wheat, rye, corn, and other farm products. We would always refer to Roy as the "Big Swede." He was a quiet kid who did not show a lot of emotion. I'm sure he missed his family and the style of life he had in Minnesota, but he never showed it. Roy was a very heavy smoker, and he loved his beer.

Our ball turret gunner found us while we were looking for him. He came from the state of Washington and his name was John "Biff" White. His family was involved in fruit orchards, mainly growing those big beautiful "Bing" cherries, and those large red and golden delicious apples. Biff was the lover on our crew, and I was sure that before the war would end, he would break many hearts. He was a very emotional person. Several times, I saw tears in his

The Lady From Hell

eyes, as he read a letter that he had received from home.

These were the enlisted men who comprised my crew, and, with the exception of John Wilson, who was several years older, we were all nineteen years old, give or take a month. We stuck together like glue. We did everything as a group. We realized that if we were going to survive this war, we would have to work together. If we did not work as a team, none of us would survive.

About a week after we had arrived at Plant Park, we were advised to pack our gear. We would be moving out to a place called Drew Field that was not very far from where we were. It would be here that we would wait for the officers of our crew to complete their training. Rumors had it that it would be several weeks before their training would be completed. We were told that it was a lack of airplanes that was causing delays.

Drew Field was strictly "Army." Many of the personnel based here were career army people, and the base itself was run strictly according to the book. I did not enjoy my stay at Drew Field. We were housed in old wooden barracks that must have been built before I was born. The streets and the walks were not paved and everything was dusty. We called it the dust bowl, except when it rained, when it became the mud bowl. It was difficult keeping the barracks, your clothing, and yourself clean under those conditions. Another thing I did not like about Drew Field was that we were assigned KP and/or guard duty every other day. Our entire purpose for staying on this dusty old base was to wait for the officers to finish their training. It was not long before the dust, mud, KP, guard duty, and boredom had us longing to be transferred out.

Finally, and with much joy, after two weeks of this drudgery, we were informed that a complete infantry division was arriving at Drew Field, and they needed the barracks we were occupying. Because of this, all air force crews were being sent to

The Lady From Hell

MacDill Field, which was not very far from Drew Field. Hopefully, we would finally meet the officers of our crew there. They were still having problems completing their training because of the lack of airplanes. Because of the huge losses in combat, the manufacturers of the airplanes were shipping them to the war zones as fast as they were being manufactured.

And so it was, with big smiles, we packed our gear, left Drew Field, and headed for MacDill Field; ever thankful we were leaving the "dust bowl." MacDill Field was a breath of fresh air. It was easily one of the most beautiful army bases that I had ever seen. The differences between Drew Field and MacDill Field were like night and day. The roads were all paved, the sidewalks were clean, and the grass areas were lush green and meticulously manicured. Our crew, in less than three weeks, had been in three different army bases, but with MacDill, we hit the jackpot. The mess halls were spotless and the food was extra tasty. Another reason I liked MacDill was because it had a beautiful ballpark. Ballparks always interested me. One day, while passing the field, I noticed a team having a practice session. I asked the sergeant in charge if I could participate in the practice. He asked me what position I played, and I replied that I was a shortstop. I was in seventh heaven when he handed me a glove, and told me to go out on the field.

Apparently, I was a success, because he sent me to the supply sergeant who outfitted me with a uniform, and told me to report at 0900 hours the next morning for batting practice. I surmised that he wanted to see if I could hit. I was nervous, but I had nothing to lose. I hit the ball as well as anyone on the team. Since I had made the team, I would be taken off future duties, and all I had to do was play ball on Mondays, Wednesdays, and Fridays! I was walking on clouds! I could not believe this was happening to me. Except to report several hours before each game, the rest of the time was my own. I continued to impress people with my arm. The skinny

The Lady From Hell

kid from Brooklyn could throw a "rope" from shortstop to first base.

I had been on the team only a week, and a lot of "firsts" were happening to me. I was playing in a ballpark that had dugouts and stands along first and third base. We were playing at night under the lights. Since most army duties were over by 1700 hours, all our games were at night. This would give the soldiers time to have dinner and come out to the park to watch us play and drink beer. I must say the stands were always full. The loud speaker would announce your name as you came to bat. It went something like this: "Playing shortstop and batting second, from Brooklyn, New York, Frank Condreras." I don't know why, but Brooklyn always got a rise out of the crowd. At any rate, I was very proud that I was playing with and against some very good professional ball players. I never realized that I could enjoy army life so much.

Unfortunately, once again, the good times were short-lived. My bubble burst when, after about a month, we were told that we would be shipping out. We were being sent to advanced combat training. We would meet our officers there. In fact, some officers had already arrived and were waiting for their crews. To say that I hated to leave would be an understatement, but unfortunately I had no choice.

11

ADVANCED COMBAT TRAINING

    For the first time since I had been in the army, our destination was not a secret. We were told we were going to Gulfport, Mississippi, where we would be taking our advanced combat training. As the army trucks arrived at the train station, I saw a big long troop train consisting of many coach cars, with the exception of the last two cars, which were Pullman sleepers. As luck would have it, the air force crews were assigned to the Pullman cars, while the infantry was put into the coach cars. It was the same infantry division that displaced us from Drew field. It seemed to me these guys never got a break. To me, those in the infantry are the heroes of all wars. I knew from previous experiences that the ride would be a long one. Troop trains take twice as long as civilian trains. I did not mind this, as our Pullman cars were as comfortable as any train car could be. I felt sorry for the infantry guys, as they could not be very comfortable in those cattle cars. We had heard they were headed to California, and the Pacific theatre of operations. Our two Pullman cars would be derailed at Biloxi, Mississippi, where army trucks would take us to Gulfport. The rest of the train would continue on to California.

At Mobile, Alabama, our train stopped for an unusually long period of time. Everyone wondered what was going on. We later found out that a soldier in one of the front cars had suffered a heart attack and had died before the medical people could get to him. How sad. I wondered how the war department would inform his loved ones that their son/husband had died of a heart attack on a troop train, before ever entering combat.

I was now starting to realize that my fun times would be coming to an end. There would be no more baseball or football games. The briefings that we had received

The Lady From Hell

at MacDill field were both loud and clear. The war and combat were very near for my crewmembers and me. After our training at Gulfport, we would be sent to the European theatre of operations. Gulfport, Mississippi would be our last American base.

The train, as we anticipated, left our two Pullman cars on some side tracks in Biloxi, where army trucks were waiting to take us to Gulfport. It was not a long ride, as the two cities were located close to each other. The greetings were almost the same at every camp. They sounded like a broken record. We were assigned barracks and bunks. We were further informed that we would have no duties until the arrival of our officers. All our bunks were equipped with huge mosquito nets, and I quickly found out why. The mosquitoes were as big as any I had ever seen, even bigger than the ones in tent city. Our barracks were located in a forest that had been recently cleared. They were still constructing more barracks when we arrived. I guess they were anticipating a long war. The latrine and shower facilities, as well as the mess hall, were located about one half mile from our barracks. It was a long walk that we made several times a day.

There was no limit to the amount of passes we received, as long as they did not interfere with our duties. I loved going to Biloxi. It was famous for its seafood, and I loved seafood. It was also the first city that I had visited that had legalized gambling. Many soldiers lost a lot of money on the Biloxi gambling runs. To be honest, until my officers arrived, I spent more time in Biloxi than I did at the base in Gulfport. It was a little more than a week before the rest of my crew arrived. We were finally going to meet our officers.

The pilot's name was Herman Meyer. He lived with his family in Washington D.C. He was of German descent and still had many relatives living in Germany. It could not have been easy for him, knowing he was going to be flying bomb runs over Germany. Herman came from a very wealthy family. It was obvious he had no money problems.

The Lady From Hell

He was twenty-six years old, making him the oldest on our crew.

Tony Dupieu was our co-pilot and was several years younger than Herman. Tony was of French descent and lived in New Orleans. He was married and was expecting his first child within the next month. How hard it must have been for him to be away from his wife at such an exciting time in their lives. Despite this hardship, Tony loved a good time and was a fun guy to be with.

"Bo" Brown was our navigator. He was single and came from Nashville, Tennessee. Bo was the most serious and learned of all the officers. He was as American as apple pie, as his ancestry dated back to the Pilgrims. He was the same age as Tony.

Last, but certainly not least, was our bombardier, Barry Robbins. He was the only crewmember of Jewish heritage. This being the case, flying over Germany during these times could certainly pose additional dangers if we were ever shot down and captured. Barry was the youngest of all the officers, and just a kid at heart. He was from Chicago, Illinois. Barry was a prankster and a comedian, and he kept our crew laughing and on our toes.

The party was now over. We were officially a complete and qualified B-17 Flying Fortress crew, and our combat training would be starting in earnest. There would be no more leaves. The next several months our crew spent more time in the air than we did on the ground. Training was very serious, intense, and continuous. We flew in the daylight, and we flew at night. We flew in formations, and we flew alone. We flew at low altitudes, and we flew at very high altitudes, making it necessary to wear oxygen masks to allow us to breathe. Many days we flew for more than eight hours. The pilots practiced landings and take-offs endlessly. We had gunnery practice all the time, shooting thousands and thousands of rounds of ammunition. If any malfunctions occurred with our guns, we corrected them in mid air. Our training was being put to good use and was certainly paying off. While

The Lady From Hell

all this was going on, I was performing my flight engineer duties. I sensed both my pilot and my co-pilot were impressed with my knowledge of the mechanical aspects of the B-17.

I was also proud of the skilled way with which I handled the top turret. I hit my targets accurately and consistently. I was feeling pretty good about myself when my instructor brought me back to reality with the remark, "It will be quite different with someone shooting back at you!" If it was his intent to instill fear into me, he succeeded. Suddenly, I was no longer cocky, and my chest had deflated considerably. Our training was almost completed, and I was quite proud of my crew. Although we were a bunch of scared kids, from all over the United States, we all knew our jobs, and performed them to the best of our abilities. Being the flight engineer, I spent a lot of time with the pilots. They were both great guys and excellent pilots. I thought the co-pilot was as good at flying the airplane as the pilot. I got to know both of them very well, and we traded many stories about our lives before the war.

About a week after the completion of our training, we received our final orders. Yes, the rumors were true. We were headed for England and the Eighth Air Force, and the war in Europe. We were being sent to Savannah, Georgia, where we would pick up a brand new Flying Fortress, just out of the factory, and fly her to England where the rest of the Eighth Air Force was already stationed. Before leaving Gulfport, I received my fourth stripe, which went under the three on top. I was now Staff Sergeant, Frank J. Condreras.

12

SAYING GOODBYE TO AMERICA

The train ride to Savannah, Georgia was definitely not a joy ride. There was concern on the faces of the entire crew. This was a civilian train. In fact, I think we were the only military people on board. The train even had a dining car, and it was nice to eat with a clean tablecloth, clean silverware, and clean glasses. It was the high point of a very somber, depressing ride. When we arrived at Savannah, the airplane we were supposed to fly to England had not yet arrived. We were advised it was not due for several days. I cannot say anything positive or negative about the city of Savannah, as we were not allowed off the base. Everything was very secretive and serious now. Every day that the plane did not arrive meant another day in the United States. This was fine with us, as it also meant one more day we avoided combat duty. Most of our time was spent playing cards and exchanging stories.

It was quite obvious that everyone missed their homes and loved ones. What I did notice was that we were doing almost everything together as a group. We were learning more and more about each other. I liked what I was seeing. Besides being a good crew, we were becoming very good friends. Our friendship would carry us through many trying times in the months to come. It was a constant comfort to have fellow crewmembers that were also friends.

On the fifth day at Savannah, someone spotted a B-17 landing. The entire crew went down to operations to get a look at this beautiful giant. She was all silver, and someone had already named her the "Sky Queen." On her nose, someone had painted a picture of a beautiful girl with a crown on her head. I went into the cockpit and checked the logbook. It was truly a new airplane. There were no mechanical problems. The only noteworthy observation

The Lady From Hell

I made was that the #2 engine used a little more fuel than the other three engines. The plane had less than thirty hours of flight time. The pilots who flew the plane to Savannah were civilian pilots who worked for the Boeing Aircraft Company. They were discussing with my pilots how well the plane had performed during the flight from Washington State, where she was made, to Savannah, Georgia.

We were to take off at 0700 hours the following morning. The mess hall food was very good, but every once in a while we would eat at the P.X. That night, all ten of us ate at the P.X. Very early the next morning all ten of us had breakfast. It would be the last meal we would have in the Untied States for a long time, possibly forever. The pilots informed us at breakfast that we would be headed for St. Johns, in Newfoundland. I did not get much sleep, because I knew there would be no turning back. This was the real thing. At 0700 hours that morning, the "Sky Queen" lifted herself off the runway at Savannah, Georgia, and we were on our way to Newfoundland. As the B-17 Flying Fortress headed north, I kept looking at the ground below. Even at twenty thousand feet, the United States looked beautiful. I prayed that some day we would all be returning to this beautiful country. Several hours later, and about three bounces later, we landed in Newfoundland. It was not the best of landings, but I had learned that any landing from which we walked away was a good landing.

We were to remain in Newfoundland until the following night. We would take off at night, and our destination would be Prestwick, Scotland. I never understood why our take-off was at night. Maybe it was so that we would be landing in Scotland in daylight hours, or maybe it was to test our navigator on his navigation skills. Whatever the reason, it was to be a night departure. We took turns guarding the airplane, two at a time, at all times. The mess hall on the base was one of the cleanest that I had ever seen. It was spotless. You could actually eat off the floors. I was impressed with the

The Lady From Hell

sign that hung over the door. It read, "Take all you want, but eat all you take." I was further impressed with the fact that there was an MP (Military Police) standing by to make sure this order was carried out. I have to say, there was very little food wasted.

This is my crew in front of "The Sky Queen." The next day we flew her to Scotland where she was picked up by a crew and put into combat.

The following evening, we left Newfoundland and headed for Prestwick, Scotland. The trip was uneventful, and the airplane performed beautifully. At daybreak, and to the relief of all of us, we spotted the Irish Coast. It was a beautiful sight. For his first night flight over water, our navigator did a superb job. He was right on the money. A little while later, we spotted the Scottish coastline. Soon thereafter, we were landing at Prestwick, Scotland. This time, the landing was beautiful – no bounces. Most of the crew did not even know we had landed. As soon as we turned off the runway, a jeep driven by the military police met us. On the jeep was a huge sign that read, "Follow me." We were lead to a restricted area where we parked the airplane. It would be the last time we saw the "Sky Queen." Shortly thereafter she would be picked up and flown to some air force base and put into combat. We heard some time later that the "Sky Queen" and her crew were shot down on a mission over Hamberg, Germany. She and her crew were on their fourth mission at the time.

Our crew spent several days in

The Lady From Hell

Prestwick, which I enjoyed. We got to play golf during the day and visit the pubs at night. We were housed in a local hotel, where we also ate our meals. But all too soon, the famous army truck arrived to take us to the train station. We boarded a train that would take us to Chelveston, England. Chelveston was located some fifty miles north of London. This would be our home for the duration of the war, or the completion of our missions, or even a combat casualty, whichever came first. The train ride took forever. It made many stops along the way, both scheduled and unscheduled. The war was having the same effect on the British railroad system as it was in the United States. When we arrived at Chelveston, our faithful army truck was waiting to take us to our base.

13

HELLO! CHELVESTON

The 305th Bomb Group was located on a huge farm. There were many cows grazing and huge haystacks all over the place. Our tail gunner, the farmer of the crew, informed us that the huge haystacks would be food for the cows during the winter months when they would be unable to graze. The Flying Fortresses were scattered on aprons all along the airfield, and not very close to one another. The truck driver had informed us that the planes were situated this way in case of a German air raid. This way, not all the planes would be destroyed. He further informed us that the last raid was several months ago. It seemed the German Air Force was more intent on bombing London and other large cities, rather than the Allied military targets. Located on the aprons, next to the Flying Fortresses, were huge tents. We would find out later that these tents contained all kinds of mechanical parts for the planes, all kinds of ammunition, and spare parts for the fifty-caliber machine guns. It was a place where the crewmembers, upon returning from a mission, would store parachutes, flak jackets, and whatever other personal items they might want to leave until their next mission. It also housed the ground crew, which consisted of a head mechanic and two assistant mechanics. There were also three cots available, in case it was necessary for the ground crew to spend the night while getting a Flying Fortress ready for flight the next day. I was told that this occurred quite frequently.

When we finally arrived at the base, the captain in charge of greeting new crews met us. He had a never-ending job, as new crews were continually arriving. He said we were assigned to the 305th Bomb Group, which consisted of four squadrons: the 364th, the 365th, the 366th, and the 422nd Bomb Squadrons. We were assigned to the 422nd Bomb Squadron. The captain advised

The Lady From Hell

us we were replacing a crew that was shot down over Germany after their fifth mission. It was a numbing thought, and I wanted to thank him for pointing this out to us. At any rate, he would meet with us the following day, and we would get a complete briefing on what was to be expected of us then. He would also take care of all our needs, such as our flight clothing and combat gear. We were assigned a barracks, as were the officers on our crew. There were six bunks for us enlisted men. The beds had already been made up with clean linens. These were the bunks that belonged to the crew that had just been shot down several days ago. It was an eerie feeling to be assigned to the bunk of a missing crewmember, and it bothered me for a long time. The barracks accommodated twenty-four crewmembers in total. We were warmly greeted by the remaining eighteen crewmembers, and soon they were exchanging war stories with us. Most of them had arrived several weeks before us. One of the crews had flown six missions while the other two had flown four missions each.

This is me standing in front of my barracks in Chelveston. This would be my new home in England.

The following day, the captain arrived at our barracks bright and early, advising us that we had an awful lot of work to do. He took us to the supply warehouse, where we were fitted for the many outfits we would need on a mission. We also received our parachute, our "Mae Wests," which were flotation devices used in case we were shot down over water, sunglasses, several different pairs of gloves, and heavy woolen boots. After all that, he gave us a tour of

The Lady From Hell

the base, including the flight operations building, the briefing room, and the hospital. The captain assured us that, if we were wounded in combat, we would receive the finest care.

The captain saved the best for last. He took us to see the airplane that would take us into combat. She was located on an apron just off one of the inactive runways. Even though she was painted in the traditional drab army green, she still looked beautiful. I also got to meet the ground crew while they were doing some work on her. The crew chief's name was John Gunn. He was from the south, which was quite obvious when he spoke. The two mechanics that worked for John were also from the south. We had an all-southern crew, and they were three of the nicest "rebels" you would ever want to meet. I liked John right away. Maybe it was the way he spoke, or maybe it was because it was obvious he loved what he was doing. Whenever he spoke of the Flying Fortress, you could tell how proud he was of her. John and I went over the logbook together. He pointed out the repairs he and his crew had made during the last few days, and what I should look for in the air. The plane had been used as a spare, which simply meant that if a crew had some kind of problem with their plane during a mission, they would use one of the spare planes for their subsequent missions. I think John was very happy that his plane now had a crew assigned to it. John had assured us that the airplane would always be ready for combat.

We now had our very own Flying Fortress, and she would be our second home, our home away from home. We were told to fly her as much as possible before our first mission. And fly her we did, sometimes ten hours a day. Each crewmember got to check out his position, his machine guns, his oxygen system, the radio, the headsets, the intercom, and many other items too numerous to mention. The airplane itself was a dream. She did everything we asked of her. We flew north, over the North Sea, and we went up to thirty-five thousand

The Lady From Hell

feet, where we could check the oxygen system and our electrically heated suits. Since temperatures can reach thirty or forty degrees below zero at those altitudes, it was important the heated suits worked properly.

Meanwhile, the pilots were putting the airplane through its paces, with a series of dives and steep turns, both right and left. The airplane handled like a dream. When we landed, John Gunn was waiting for us. I had written nothing in the logbook, since everything went so well. John and his crew were already on ladders, checking oil consumption on all four engines before we had even gotten into the jeep, which was waiting to take us back to the barracks. I would find out before the end of the war that there was no better mechanic in the Air Force than John Gunn. His crew would say that he was born with a wrench in his hand. We were indeed very lucky to have him.

Frank J. Condreras

My buddies and I are sitting atop an air raid shelter, not far from my barracks.

The next day, we had a meeting with the commanding officer of the 422nd Squadron. He welcomed us and told us that if we needed or wanted anything at all, all we had to do was ask. He went over several procedures that he indicated we would need to know. For example, if we should get shot down, we were to give only our name, rank, and serial number. He also advised us to stay away from the civilian

The Lady From Hell

population as well, because they were so incensed at the Allied Air Forces for bombing and killing their loved ones, that they would pose a greater threat to the American soldier than the German military. In addition, if we were assigned to participate in a mission, it would be posted on the bulletin board the night before, and we were to tie a white towel on our bunks, so the company clerk would know who needed to be awakened.

All missions started early in the morning. As long as we were not on a mission, our time would be our own. We had unlimited pass privileges. I guess we were as ready as we would ever be. We were dismissed and left to wait for our first mission. The commanding officer's last words were, "Be proud Americans. You are flying the finest heavy bomber in the world. Take care of it, and it will take care of you. God bless you all, and God speed." We left his office, and we returned to our barracks to wait.

14

MY FIRST MISSION

During that first briefing with our commanding officer we were told that, upon the completion of twenty-five missions, we would be sent home. I will not try to describe all my missions, as circumstances can make it very difficult to obtain the necessary information from the appropriate resources, and it is not my intent to make this a history book. The missions flown by the United States Army Eighth Air Force can be found in the many history books that have been published since the war's end. Therefore, my descriptions here would be both repetitious and boring. Instead, I will describe things that I remember. They are things that are not found in the history books, but in the memories and hearts of those of us who flew in these missions during combat, again and again. First let me say that all missions flown by the Eighth Air Force, over Germany and German occupied territories, basically followed the same procedure. While the targets and the types of bombs that were carried may have differed from mission to mission, all missions started the same way. Sometimes, the endings differed. Unfortunately, many crews never made it back to the base.

    We began by checking the bulletin board on a daily basis. Mission information was usually posted as soon as it was received. This was how it all started. When the 305th Bomb Group was involved, we needed to check to see which of the four squadrons was assigned to participate. Sometimes, missions required sending up two squadrons, sometimes three. Whenever the mission called for a maximum effort, all four squadrons would be airborne. Usually, when all four squadrons were needed, it would mean that one of the larger cities in Germany would be the intended target. We'd been in Chelveston for about three or four days when the announcements on the

The Lady From Hell

bulletin board indicated our squadron was to participate in a three-squadron mission. It was the first mission for our crew, and, needless to say, I felt sick and scared. All my training had not prepared me for these feelings.

All missions started early in the morning. The reason for this was that the Eighth Air Force wanted to bomb the intended targets between the hours of eleven o'clock in the morning and one o'clock in the afternoon. This time frame disrupted the lunch hour of the German population, and carrying out missions at these times was done strictly for psychological reasons. On the morning of our first mission, we were awakened at four o'clock in the morning. I did not sleep well the night before. I tossed and turned all night long, so it was almost a relief when the company clerk came in to tell us it was time. As the flight engineer, it was my job to make sure the rest of my crew was up. It was the pilot's responsibility to get the officers up. No one had slept well, so we were ready to go when the truck rolled up to our barracks at four thirty to take us to the mess hall. The mess hall was located about a mile from our barracks. For breakfast, we could have anything we wanted, including eggs, pancakes, French toast, waffles, and all sorts of goodies. If you asked, the cooks would even cook you up a steak. Not many of us had the stomach for steak that early in the morning. In fact, there were many crewmembers who did not eat anything, but rather just drank coffee. As for me, I always ate well. I was nervous, I was scared, and I was tired. But I was also hungry. We were told to eat a hearty breakfast, so if we were shot down during the mission, at least we would have a full stomach. Food could be mighty scarce if we had to bail out over Germany.

After breakfast, the same truck that had taken us to the mess hall now took us to the briefing hut. A truck was assigned to each crew, and it would remain with that crew right until the time it delivered us to the apron where our airplane was parked. The briefing building was a large hut, which

The Lady From Hell

could seat many crewmembers. When all crewmembers were inside and seated, the MPs secured and locked all doors. No one could either enter or leave until the briefing was over. Over the front wall hung a huge blanket, which covered a large map of England and the rest of Europe. The briefing officer began the briefing by removing the blanket, revealing three sets of yarn running from London to the intended targets of the day. There were lots of moans and groans that could be heard at this time. Some crewmembers coughed to clear their throats. Others got sick and vomited. Still, the briefing went on. The sets of yarn were three different colors. A red string indicated our primary target and the route we would take to get there. A blue string indicated our secondary target and route, and a white string indicated our third and last choice. It was clear to us that we were going to be spending long hours over Germany and German occupied territories.

The briefing officer advised us that there would be several points where we could expect the Luftwaffe to hit us, both before and after we'd reached our intended target. He also advised us to expect heavy concentrations of anti-aircraft fire around the target area. The primary target for my first mission was the manufacturing plants and oil refineries located in the city of Merseburg. Our escort fighters would accompany us as far as their range would allow. Unfortunately, this was not very far. We would be by ourselves a good part of the mission. As soon as the briefing officer finished, the weather officer took over and briefed us on any weather problems we might encounter. Last, but not least, our group commander would give us his "Go get them!" speech, which would conclude with, "Make the 305th Bomb Group proud!"

The truck drivers, who waited patiently throughout our breakfast and briefing, then took us to the apron where our plane was parked. The apron, at this time, was a "bee-hive" of activity. The ground crew was performing their last minute duties. A fuel truck pulled up and one of the mechanics

The Lady From Hell

topped off the fuel tanks, making sure each was filled to capacity. Soon after, the oil truck pulled up and another mechanic checked the oil on each engine. Everyone had his job, and he would do it to perfection. There was no room for error in situations like this. Meanwhile, the armor people were busy loading bombs into the bomb bays. As we were told in the briefing, we would be carrying ten of the five-hundred pound bombs. The crew was the busiest of all. I brought my parachute up first, and laid it near the hatch opening near the nose of the B-17. This way, if I had to bail out, my parachute would be readily available. I then laid my flak jacket at the base of my top turret. We were supposed to wear these jackets, but they were so heavy and cumbersome that I would rather take my chances. I also made sure I had my full complement of fifty-caliber ammunition. It would be the crewmember's responsibility to "belt" his own ammunition as he saw fit. I would use two armor-piercing bullets, two incendiaries, and a flare bullet. The flare was not very accurate, but it was very visible, and it would remind the German pilots that I was aware of their presence. I also took one hundred rounds, maybe two hundred, more than I was supposed to, for each gun. Most crewmembers did the same. Everyone was busy checking out his position and making sure his guns were free and clear of any problems. Meanwhile, the navigator was mapping out the best route for our return flight, should we get separated from our squadron. The bombardier was overseeing the loading of the bombs onto the plane, and the pilots were doing a last minute inspection of the cockpit. As for me, I was reviewing my final checkpoints with John Gunn, our lead mechanic.

The Lady From Hell

This was the top turret of the B-17 Flying Fortress, where I spent many anxious hours scanning the skies for enemy aircraft.

When all the preparatory work was done, we piled into the airplane, and waited for our orders. During takeoff, the pilots and I were in the cockpit, the bombardier and navigator were in the nose, and the rest of the crew sat either in the radio room or in the waist. We ran our engines to give them a last minute check, and then shut down to wait for the order to take off. We waited for what seemed like forever, until finally the word came. Three groups, consisting of thirty-six Flying Fortresses moved out, forming a single line as we approached the runway. As we were approaching the runway, we went through our checklist of procedures. Finally, we were next in line to take off. We set the brakes, ran the engines up to full capacity, and then released the brakes. The plane lunged forward and started down the runway. My first mission had begun. I called out the airspeed, and when we reached one hundred to one hundred and ten miles per hour, the pilot pulled back on the yoke. The plane took a little longer than usual to take off. It was loaded with a full complement of bombs, full fuel tanks, ten crewmembers, thirteen fifty-caliber machine guns, and more ammunition than was permitted. Despite all this, our Flying Fortress was now airborne, having cleared the trees at the end of the runway with ease. For the next several minutes, we were flying through clouds, and when we finally broke through the clouds and into the sunlight, it was a sight to behold. There were Flying Fortresses all over the sky,

The Lady From Hell

each looking for their groups while trying to get into formation as quickly as possible. Finding your group and quickly getting into formation saved a lot of fuel, which could eventually be of critical importance at the end of your mission. It was indeed a beautiful sight, to see six or seven hundred Flying Fortresses heading out for the day's target over Germany. I wondered, "How many of us would return?" We would soon find out.

As the formations headed out over the English Channel, we picked up our fighter escorts. They were composed of P-51 and P-47 aircraft. These two fighter escorts were, without a doubt, the best in the world. Unfortunately, they did not have the range to escort the big bombers deep into Germany. The Luftwaffe, using its Focke-Wulf and Messerschmidt airplanes, would just wait for our escorts to leave, before they started their attacks. During this mission, the Luftwaffe hit the formations in front and in back. The 305th Bomb Group was flying in the middle of this formation, and we only got the tail end of the attacking Messerschmidts. We were lucky. That was until we came to the target. The sky was actually black with flak. You could hear it hitting the plane. It sounded like hail hitting your car. As we started our bomb run, the bomb bay doors were opened, and as I looked down from my top turret position, I could see the city of Merseburg below. I could see flak all over the sky, and I could see the bombs from the preceding groups hitting the ground. This is the part of the mission where the bombardier takes control of the plane and advises that we are starting our bomb run. The minutes during which it takes him to glide the plane towards the target feel like an eternity. Then we hear the famous words, "Bombs away!"

The Lady From Hell

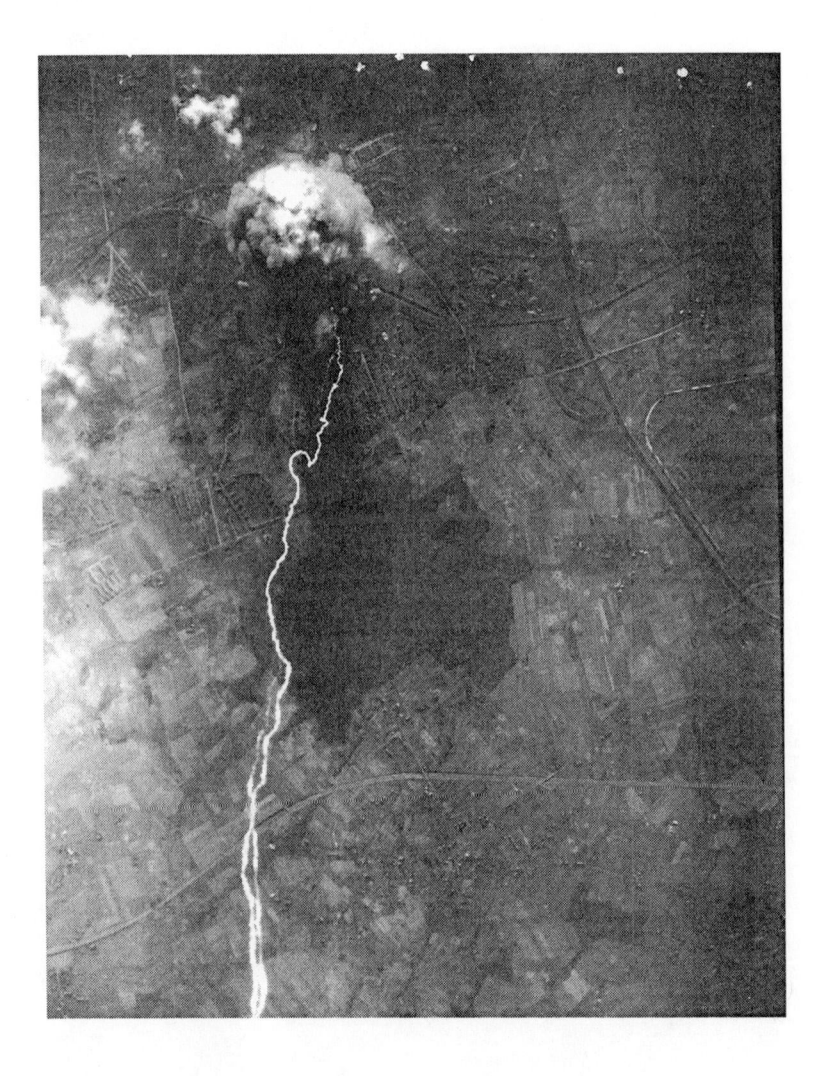

Bombs from the preceding group hitting the target area.

As soon as our bombs were released, the pilot put the airplane into a dive, which, at times, would cause the airspeed to reach over two hundred and fifty miles per hour. I know that by today's standards that is not very fast. However, for a heavy bomber, at that time, it was very fast. There were two reasons for the Flying Fortress to dive away from the target area after the release of the bombs. First, we wanted to get out of the flak area as quickly as possible, and second, we wanted to get out of the way of the following groups dropping their bombs. I saw some Fortresses that had been hit by flak. One was on fire, and as it started down, I counted the number of parachutes I saw opening. Hoping for ten, I only counted four as the plane disappeared into the clouds below. Another Fortress went into a spin and rapidly descended into the clouds. I saw no chutes open. Although our plane sustained its share of hits, we were lucky enough to remain airborne and stay in formation.

As we headed back home from the target, our formations were very close. The lead plane determined the speed and

The Lady From Hell

altitude at which the entire formation flew. Sometimes, the planes came mighty close to each other, with wings narrowly missing one another. The pilots had to constantly be on alert, but there were times when collisions occurred. More than a few planes were lost in this manner, but flying in such close formation allowed for more concentrated firepower when retaliating against attacking planes. Unfortunately, this would also increase the risk of shooting each other, in an attempt to fight off German fighters. The German fighters would use the tactic of flying directly in the path of the sun, making it difficult to detect their presence, and come barreling through our formations. Many planes were lost as a result of these maneuvers as well.

Although the Luftwaffe showed up on our return trip, they never attacked the formation. Maybe they did not want to risk any more losses, or maybe they were running low on fuel or ammunition. For whatever reason, I was most grateful.

About an hour after hitting our target,

the formation started to descend to lower altitudes. I was always happy to remove my oxygen mask, which I had been wearing for more than four hours. Because of the below-zero temperatures, the perspiration would cause the mask to freeze to your face, leaving a mark that stayed with you several hours after landing. It was the reason most of us looked like raccoons after a mission. The B-17 was not a pressurized aircraft. In fact, it was wide open, and at high altitudes, temperatures of thirty, forty and fifty degrees below zero were not uncommon. Frostbite was one of our biggest enemies.

Needless to say, we were greatly relieved when we saw our fighter escorts, with those great big beautiful stars on their wings. Suddenly, the Luftwaffe was gone. They wanted no part of our fighters. As our escorts appeared, the formations loosened up considerably. From what I could see, by the holes in the formations, we had lost quite a few Flying Fortresses. I would later find out that the Eighth Air Force acknowledged that forty-eight planes

The Lady From Hell

had been shot down and many more had sustained damages. Flak was one of the biggest culprits. The Germans protected their manufacturing plants well, because without them the war would have ended very quickly.

As we approached our airfield, the weather was clear. Several planes shot their flares, as was the custom when returning from a mission. Certain colors indicated that there were wounded on board, while others indicated mechanical problems. These planes had priority and would be the first ones to land. We had some holes in our plane, but no mechanical problems and, fortunately, no casualties. We would be one of the last to land. It didn't matter to me. We had returned from our first mission.

As we taxied toward our apron, our ground crew was there to greet us. With thumbs up, they guided the pilots to park the airplane in its proper position. I wish I could describe what a wonderful feeling it was when I jumped out of the nose of the airplane and my feet touched the ground. I

Frank J. Condreras

had just completed my first mission, and I was back, and I was alive. I would brag to anyone that would listen. We just had our first taste of combat, and we had returned! The only thing that put a damper on this joyous occasion was the fact that we would have to do this twenty-four more times.

This is me with my ground crew. There was no better ground crew anywhere. That's the "Lady" off to the right.

I talked with John Gunn, reviewing what I had written in the logbook. They were all minor problems, as the airplane had performed beautifully in combat. As I spoke, I could see a big smile light up John's

The Lady From Hell

face. He was very proud. It was quite obvious that we were both in love with the same Flying Fortress. The damage we had sustained from the anti-aircraft guns and enemy fighters was minimal. There were several holes on the side of the plane and in the tail section as well. John assured us that these could be fixed in no time at all. As we were talking, a Red Cross truck pulled up to our apron with coffee and donuts. The coffee hit the spot, and the donuts, well, I had three of them. Enough said! The Red Cross people continued to be my favorite people. I can still remember them in the United States. Whenever the troop train would make stops, they would always be there, and they did it for the love of their country. They were not paid, and it was sometimes a thankless job. God bless each and every one of them. Finally, the truck arrived at the apron to take us back to where we had started the day, the large briefing hut. This hut was also where we would have our debriefings after our missions.

Frank J. Condreras

Before we entered the briefing hut, two sergeants, standing behind a makeshift bar, handed all the crewmembers a double shot of scotch. Almost all of us accepted this drink, even those of us who did not drink. I sipped mine. It felt good. It calmed my nerves and warmed my stomach. I kept thinking that if I completed my twenty-five missions, I would have consumed twenty-five double shots of scotch. That's well over a bottle. Mom would never believe this. As we entered the hut with drinks in hand, we were led to one of the empty tables. Behind the table sat a captain and a sergeant who would be taking notes. There were about six tables which would accommodate all the crews. Crews would arrive at different times, so sometimes there would be a waiting period to get in.

We started to explain our mission: Yes, we were hit by enemy fighters. No, they were not Focke-Wulfs, but Messerschmidts. Yes, the 305th was lucky, as these enemy fighters only made a few passes at us, and then left. Yes, I did get some shots off, but

The Lady From Hell

I don't think I hit them, as they came from underneath the plane, and I did not have time to adjust my turret or my sights on them. I was sure the film would show all this. Cameras were mounted on each turret, and as we fired our guns, the camera was activated and began filming. It was in this way that the damage to enemy aircraft was monitored and verified.

As the captain interviewed each crewmember, each version would be a little different, depending on the position from which the guns were fired. We questioned the captain on the extremely heavy flak we had encountered over the target. It was certainly a lot heavier than they had indicated during the morning briefing. The captain did not have an answer, but he assured us he would find out and let us know. I really did not care at this point. I was feeling good, not only because the interrogation was over, but also because I was now feeling the effects of the double scotch.

The trucks that had been assigned to

us all day now took us back to our barracks. I was starting to get ready to go to the mess hall with John, my radio operator, when I decided to lay down a few minutes before eating. The next thing I knew, it was seven o'clock the next morning, and John was waking me up for breakfast. When I asked him why he did not wake me up for last night's dinner, he said that I was sleeping so soundly that he did not have the heart to wake me up. He threw a blanket over me, so that I would not freeze to death, and he went to dinner alone. What can I say about John that I haven't already said? He was a true friend, and I was fortunate to have him on my crew. Together, we headed to the mess hall for breakfast.

The Lady From Hell

This picture of our crew was taken after our very first mission.

Before the war's end, I would have witnessed and participated in some of the most vicious aerial combat ever staged. They had an intensity never matched, even in the theatre. I have seen airplanes colliding in mid-air. I have seen tail sections and wings completely shot off. I have seen Flying Fortresses disintegrate in mid-air, after receiving a direct hit. I have seen two

Frank J. Condreras

Fortresses flying in close formation, when their wings collided and both planes went spinning towards the earth in flames. I have also seen planes returning from a raid so badly damaged that they would never fly again. However, the saddest sight of all was the removal of injured crew members from these planes, sometimes in pieces. It was never a pretty sight.

15

THE LADY FROM HELL

As I was returning from breakfast the day after our first mission, there was a message summoning me to company headquarters as soon as possible. I couldn't imagine why I would be called to company headquarters, but I soon found out. I was receiving a promotion and, with it, another stripe. I was now a Technical Sergeant, with two stripes under three. I kept thinking what a long journey it had been from that first day in Fort Dix, when a scared, hungry and cold kid lay in a narrow cot, unable to sleep. Even on this day, I was still scared, but I was no longer hungry or cold, and I was quite proud of what I had accomplished. There were several other "happenings" after our first mission.

The first was when our entire crew received the Air Medal. I don't know why

Frank J. Condreras

we received this medal after our first mission because usually a crew would fly several missions before receiving this medal, but who was I to disagree with our company commander? I didn't make the rules. I just followed them to the best of my ability. Our company commander read our citation, which went something like this:

> For meritorious achievements, while participating in bomber-sustained combat operations over Germany and German-occupied territories; the calmness and coolness displayed by these enlisted men on this occasion reflects great credit and glory upon themselves and their country.
>
> A very grateful nation thanks you.

I'm not sure if the wording is exact since it's been a very long time, but I should have remembered this citation by heart, since I would be receiving it four more times before the end of the war.

Another thing that happened was that we were now allowed to wear a piece of blue material under our wings, on the left side of our uniform. This indicated that

The Lady From Hell

we were active flight personnel engaged in combat duty. A lot of nice things were beginning to happen, and if the war had ended at that time, everything would have been perfect.

"The Lady From Hell" flying right wing (at the bottom of the picture).

Later that day, I borrowed a jeep and went down to look at my favorite Flying Fortress. There she stood, as proud as could be. Her holes had already been patched up, just as John, our lead mechanic, had promised. As a crew, we had all agreed on a name for our plane. We were going to call her "The Lady From Hell." We thought this name would be appropriate since she had taken us to hell and back on our very first mission, and we were hoping she would be bringing us back from hell many more times. We were having a picture of a beautiful girl with flaming red hair, wearing a red dress, and holding a pitchfork in her hand, painted on the right side of the nose. The very next day, the painter had finished, and had done a terrific job. She was just beautiful. Also painted on the left side of the nose, was the picture of one bomb, indicating our first mission. Soon there would be many more, and she was now ready for our second mission.

During the next two weeks, we flew five missions targeting the cities of Frankfurt, Hamburg, Hanover, Saarbrucken, and, once again, Merseburg. In the Merseburg briefing we were told that, in our last raid, we had missed most of the intended targets. They admitted to us that this was due to the heavy concentration of flak that had disrupted the bomb run. This time, however, we would be bombing at a much higher altitude, and this would hopefully help us reach our intended targets successfully. I had remembered Merseburg well, as it was our first mission, and we had lost a lot of planes. I was hoping that the second time around would be different, and that we would return unharmed as we did before. The missions followed a familiar pattern. Enemy fighters would hit us before and after the target area. Over the target area, the flak was murderous. I learned to hate flak more than the enemy fighters. At least you could shoot back at a fighter. You could do nothing about flak but sit there and wait to get hit.

Maybe the British were right in their thoughts that flying over Germany for long periods of time in broad daylight was suicidal. The Luftwaffe was just too strong, and the anti-aircraft fire on visible targets would spell disaster on the bomber crews. The Royal Air Force had tried, but after sustaining tremendous losses, they abandoned the idea, and flew their missions at night.

Since we were over Germany for such long periods of time, the Luftwaffe had ample time to hit our formations over and over again. We did fairly well in missions two, three, and four, as we held our own. I, myself, hit several German fighters, and at least they knew we were there waiting for them. The problem was that they also hit us. Although we were hitting our targets, we were paying a heavy price. At times our losses were greater than ten percent, which meant that one out of every ten airplanes would not return from a mission. Many of those that did return were badly damaged and carried wounded crewmembers. We tried flying different box formations, concentrating as much firepower as possible. Flying in close formations always helped. On our second Merseburg run, we were hit by flak and lost

The Lady From Hell

our #2 engine. Since there was no fire, we were able to shut it down immediately. It happened right after we had released our bombs. With only three engines, we could not keep up with the formation, and we were dropping further and further behind the pack. We knew we would be easy prey for the Luftwaffe should they spot us but, as luck would have it, the Luftwaffe had apparently had enough for that day.

When a bomber is damaged, either by enemy fighters or anti-aircraft fire, the crew is on its own. The squadron cannot wait or slow down to accommodate a damaged airplane, as this might endanger the entire group. This was the type of situation on which the Luftwaffe thrived. We were fortunate that day that they had turned in early.

After what seemed like an eternity, the first fighters we sighted were the American P-51s. What beautiful sight to see. They stayed with us until we spotted the English Channel and the White Cliffs of Dover, and then they dipped their wings and left. We could have landed at the White Cliffs of Dover, an airfield used in emergencies for any allied airplanes, and which lay right in front of us. However, our three engines were performing so well that we decided to try and get back to our base in Chelveston. About one hour later, we finally landed, to find out that the rest of our group had already returned hours earlier.

Because we were so late getting back to base, we missed the Red Cross truck, and the truck that brought us to the debriefing was late as well. Maybe it was for the best because it gave me a chance to go over the problems we had encountered on our mission with John Gunn. This time there were quite a few, and John and his ground crew were going to be pretty busy the next few days.

The Lady From Hell

The "Lady" being inspected for damage that occurred during a mission.

Our debriefing didn't take very long. Our group had lost six airplanes. The 422nd Squadron had lost two of the planes, and they were both from the barracks right next to us. Guys with whom we were playing ball, eating, laughing, and joking just the day before, were no longer around. And they were not going to be around, ever again. It was an eerie feeling. The 422nd Squadron was like a morgue. No one said too much. You swallowed hard and life would go on, if you were lucky. Replacement crews and airplanes were on their way, and in a few days we would fly another mission. Again, there would be crews who would not be returning. It would never end. It would continue as a vicious cycle until the end of the war.

Despite the gloom and doom of the day, we also had some good news. Two of my crewmembers had received telegrams from the United States. Within one week of each other, our radio operator and our co-pilot had become the proud fathers of beautiful bouncing baby girls. John's girl weighed 7 pounds 6 ounces, and Tony's girl weighed 7 pounds 10 ounces. We treated both fathers to the best dinner we could find in London.

16

FINALLY, THE P-51s

Before our arrival at Chelveston, the 305th Bomb Group had participated in two raids on the city of Schweinfurt. Both raids were disastrous. The Eighth Air Force and the 305th Bomb Group, in particular, had suffered heavy losses. Schweinfurt had plants that manufactured ball and roller bearings, and these plants were located in the heart of the city. The first of the two missions took place on August 17, 1943. The 305th lost only two Flying Fortresses on this mission. The second raid over Schweinfurt which took place on October 14, 1943, would have quite a different outcome.

The veterans based at the 305th Bomb Group called it "Black Thursday," and rightfully so. According to the records, eighteen B-17 Flying Fortresses took off in very inclement weather. Three of these planes aborted shortly after takeoff, leaving fifteen Flying Fortresses to participate in the mission. Many of them never made it to the target. The Luftwaffe, with its Messerschmitts, was the reason. According to the records, only three Flying Fortresses made it to the target, and one of them was in flames when it dropped its bombs. Only two returned to base at the end of the day. The toll from this mission was staggering. Forty men died, twenty were wounded, and some seventy became prisoners of war. It seemed like it could not get any blacker than "Black Thursday." Maybe bombing Germany in daylight, over long periods of time, without any escorts, was suicide.

Our losses at the 305th were the heaviest ever suffered by a bomb group. Somewhere along the line, the Eighth Air Force had miscalculated the strength of the German defenses, both on the ground and in the air. The 88-millimeter anti-aircraft guns were the finest anti-aircraft guns in

The Lady From Hell

the world. These guns fired very quickly, were very accurate, and very devastating when they hit an aircraft. This, coupled with the best radar system in the war, made life very miserable for the bomber crews. On several missions, the Eighth Air Force countered their radar by dropping boxes of 'chaf' out of the bombers. Chaf is the same as the tinsel that is used to decorate Christmas trees. Just before the target, the chaf would be released handfuls at a time, and as they hit the air, they would hit each other causing the German radar to jam. This worked for three or four missions before the Germans got wise to it.

Of course, there was still the Luftwaffe. They were capable of attacking the formations at any time before and after the bombing of a target. The writing was on the wall. The big, slow, heavy bombers could not go deep into Germany unescorted, without sustaining heavy losses. So, it came to pass that many planes were lost on the Schweinfurt raids, as well as other raids that were flown without escorts. The losses sustained in the Schweinfurt raids were particularly heavy. According to reports, the Eighth Air Force lost sixty B-17s and crew casualties amounted to over 600 men. The Eighth Air Force was forced to suspend operations for a short time, until they could regroup and secure more planes and more crews from the United States. These reinforcements would enable them to continue the bombings, which was their primary concern. They did not seem overly concerned with the tremendous loss of human life.

I must relay a story involving Major General Collins, commander of the 42nd Rainbow Infantry Division, as it took place before the end of the war. This Rainbow Division had captured Schweinfurt and the Nazi flag that flew over City Hall. Major General Collins sent the captured flag to Major General Spaatz, commander of the Eighth Air Force. Because of its heavy losses, General Spaatz, in turn, sent the flag to the 305th Bomb Group. There was an inscription on the flag that read, "The

The Lady From Hell

Rainbow Division has avenged your losses at Schweinfurt." Tears welled up in my eyes, as I read the inscription. Before the Rainbow Division captured the city of Schweinfurt, it would be bombed many more times. Most of the city lay in ruins, and would stay that way for a long time. Maybe all those lives that were lost by the Eighth Air Force were not in vain. I'm sure the Rainbow Division would have suffered many more losses, had it not been for the Eighth Air Force.

Still, flying unescorted into Germany was a real liability. We had heard rumors that the P-51 fighters were being fitted with fuel tanks in the wing tips and rear fuselage. This would allow the fighters to escort our bombers all the way into Germany and back. As soon as they encountered enemy fighters, the P-51s would drop their wing tip tanks and be ready to engage the enemy. I wanted to be around when this happened. I wanted to be a part of these escorted raids. I only wish I could have seen the expressions on the faces of the

Luftwaffe pilots when they came up to hit our formations and found the P-51s flying side by side with the big bombers. There would be no more easy pickings.

My seventh, eighth, and ninth missions included raids over the cities of Hanover, Frankfurt, and, for the third time, Merseburg. Although the rumors regarding the escorts persisted, these missions were also unescorted. Several groups claimed they saw some P-51s flying along side of the formations, quite deep into Germany. My tenth mission was a Berlin raid. During the briefing, we were informed that we were going to have escort fighters accompany us the entire trip into Berlin, and, upon the completion of the bomb run, they would be waiting to escort us back to base. I had never heard a louder cheer in my life than what erupted from the crewmembers after that announcement. The raid on Berlin was mind-boggling. Over one thousand B-17 Flying Fortresses and B-24 Liberators were involved. Never in my life did I see a sky so full of airplanes scurrying to get into

The Lady From Hell

formations. There were a lot of near misses, as group after group started out towards Germany and its capital city of Berlin.

Somewhere over Belgium, we met our escort. What a sight to behold. The beautiful P-51s, in their silver splendor, with their wing tip tanks, were flying along side of us, below us, and above us. What a good feeling. The Luftwaffe was in for quite a shock. Perhaps they even suspected something, because we did not encounter them until we were quite deep into Germany. It was only then that we heard the words "Bandits in the area," which meant that one of the aircraft had spotted enemy fighters. It was usually the lead aircraft that would spot the enemy bandits first, although there were times when a gunner would see them before anyone else. No matter who spotted them and alerted the rest of the formation, these words usually instilled fear into our hearts and knots into the pits of our stomachs. This time, however, it was a little different. We were a little more at ease, thanks to our escorts.

Frank J. Condreras

The "Lady" returning from a mission with a P-51 Mustang flying off her right wing.

As soon as the word came, the P-51 wing tip tanks were dropped, and the dog fights started. It was a sight you might only see in movies, or maybe in the newsreels. While some German fighters did manage to break through, they were only able to make one or two passes before they were hit by the P-51s. There was no doubt in my mind that the P-51 was the superior airplane, and that the American pilot was the superior pilot. This was the case on that particular day, and on many days to follow. There was also no doubt in my mind about who was ruling the sky. I saw a lot of planes being shot down that day, and most of them were German fighters. The Luftwaffe was not in the habit of attacking the bomber formations during the actual bomb run, and with good reason. The flak was murderous, and they could easily have been shot down by their own anti-aircraft fire. This gave me a chance to get out of my top turret for a little while. Usually, I would stand between the pilot and co-pilot and check out the instrument panel, making sure all gauges were operating within a safe range. The pilots were busy enough, just trying to stay in formation. During the bomb run, both pilots were usually sweating profusely. Timing was of the essence, because if your plane fell behind the formation, the group above you could have easily hit you when they released their bombs.

As we started our bomb run over Berlin, the sky was full of flak. The escort left us just before we entered the bomb run and the anti-aircraft gunners were doing a job on us. Still, wave upon wave of B-24 and B-

17 bombers were dropping tons of bombs. The sky was actually black from the flak that was being shot up at us, and the bombs that were dropping out of the bellies of the giant bombers. As I looked down through the bomb bay, I could see the bombs from the previous group hitting the ground. It seemed like a never-ending bombardment, with thousands upon thousands of five-hundred pound bombs exploding as they hit the ground. We were told that there were more bombs being dropped on this one raid than the German Air Force would drop on England during the entire war. As the bombers kept coming, dropping load after load, Berlin became a huge fireball. As far as the eye could see, the entire city was on fire. "Oh God," I wondered, "how can anyone survive this?"

The Germans protected their capital city fiercely. The Luftwaffe was relentless in their attacks. The fighters that had succeeded in breaking through our escort went mostly after the B-24 groups. During this raid, losses to both sides were tremendous. Most of the losses to our heavy bombers occurred over Berlin, which was the only place the fighter escorts could not accompany us. Our losses were due to the heavy concentration of flak over the city. Basically, this was the only place we sustained significant losses during the entire raid. Our escorts certainly proved effective in protecting us during the rest of the mission. After this raid, the Luftwaffe certainly knew they would be in a battle of survival from this point on. They suffered a tremendous loss of aircraft, as our P-51s had done a job on them. Unfortunately, our losses were great as well. The government estimated that fifty bombers had failed to return that day. They conveniently forgot to mention that five hundred men also failed to return. Among those five hundred men were six with whom I had shared a meal the night before. I had seen quite a few Flying Fortresses go down over the target area, and in one of those was the crew from my barracks. When we got back, we saw six empty bunks. Their belongings had already been moved to the "death barracks" where, eventually, their possessions would be returned to their loved ones. In a day or two, a replacement crew would arrive, and the war would continue. My crew was very fortunate to have returned that day. That Berlin raid was intense, yet we escaped with very little damage, and what damage we did sustain was from the heavy flak.

    The feeling around the Eighth Air Force was that we had broken the back of the Luftwaffe. The tremendous air raids over the big cities of Germany in 1944, including the last raid over Berlin, were devastating to the Luftwaffe. Not only did they lose massive numbers of fighters, but also many German aces as well. In our briefing after the Berlin raid, we were told that over one hundred and fifty enemy aircraft were destroyed, including some thirty to forty German aces. There would still be German resistance against the bombers, and the anti-aircraft fire would still be as fierce, however, the tide had clearly turned. It was no longer the Luftwaffe that ruled

The Lady From Hell

the skies over Germany. It was now our sky, and it belonged to the United States Army's Eighth Air Force.

The arrival of the P-51 escorts did not eliminate all of our problems, however. The bombings of German cities would continue until the end of the war. There would be many subsequent raids when we would go into Germany unescorted. Weather problems, mechanical problems, miscommunications, requests from army ground forces, or last minute target changes would cause us to miss the escorts. On most of these occasions, the Luftwaffe would show, make a few tentative passes at the bombers, and then disappear, almost as if they were afraid our escorts would show up unexpectedly.

Our very next mission was a Hanover raid, and we encountered no problems. Although we had no fighter escort on this raid, the Luftwaffe never bothered us. The thing that we found bothersome was the extreme cold. We had to bomb at extremely high altitudes, and the temperature was fifty degrees below zero. Thank God for our electrically heated flying suits, which helped maintain our bodies at life-sustaining temperatures. Oxygen was also a problem at these brutally cold temperatures. The vapor from your breath would collect in the hose that came from the tank, and freeze. We had to keep squeezing the hose to keep it from icing up and occluding the passageway. The morphine in the medical kit presented an additional problem, as it could easily freeze at these temperatures. I would usually tape a vial under my armpit to prevent this from happening. Morphine was kept on board in case someone was wounded, as it could be injected immediately to help kill the pain.

    I've mentioned only a few of the many problems that could potentially arise during a mission, or the preparation thereof. In addition to these, problems could arise pursuant to a takeoff or landing. As I have previously stated, inclement weather could easily delay your formation and cause you to miss your escort. You could encounter

The Lady From Hell

problems during the loading of the bombs and ammunition. Finally, and certainly worth mentioning, the difficulty you encountered when trying to locate your group during takeoff, while many planes were trying to do the same thing, posed a great deal of danger. Even once you found your group, your problems were not over, as your pilot had to keep the plane in tight formation all the way to the target and back. More than one plane was lost when wings of adjacent planes came into contact with each other and caused both planes to lose control. In short, there were many problems that could cause your demise before you ever saw combat. Needless to say, a "milk run," which implied an "easy" mission, did not always mean you would make it back to base. Too many lives were lost during these "milk runs."

    The Frankfurt raid was a little different. We had a small group of fighter escorts, but nothing like the Berlin raid. All I saw was three or four groups of P-51 fighters. Maybe they assigned the escort according to the difficulty of the mission, or the number of bombers on the mission. The number of bombers on the Frankfurt raid was less than one third of those on the Berlin raid, but nevertheless, it was a comfort to see the P-51s in the air next to us. During the bomb run over Frankfurt, one of the shells exploded right under our plane, and it lifted our plane several hundred feet in the air. It was so close that I heard the shell explode. Several pieces of shrapnel pierced our cockpit, hitting our hydraulic tank and causing the fluid to spill out. This meant that anything operated hydraulically would not function. Our biggest problem was that we would have no brakes for our landing, which we hoped we would be doing under our own powers. Fortunately, we found ourselves returning from this mission with damage to only our hydraulic tank. Without brakes, we decided to land at the White Cliffs of Dover, where extra long runways could accommodate the extended stopping distances when a plane had lost its brakes. After all, these runways were

The Lady From Hell

used for occasions such as this, and we did not have many choices at this time. So, when we spotted the English coastline, we broke away from our formation and headed for Dover. The pilot made a normal landing, and whatever fluid was left in the lines slowed the plane down to an extent. We gradually rolled to a stop, a long way from where we had first touched down. Within minutes, a jeep with a tow bar showed up, and towed us to a huge hangar. They replaced our hydraulic tank and the fluid we had lost. The next day we were on our way back to our base. I began to realize how increasingly lucky we were each time we were able to return to base.

Some days after the Frankfurt raid, a new crew arrived in our barracks. This was the replacement crew for the one we had lost in the Berlin raid. They reminded me so much of my own crew, it was uncanny. Like us, they arrived from the United States, via Scotland. Like us, they were very young and very scared. Their first mission was to be Merseburg, just as ours had been several months ago. Our crews had a lot in common, and since we were now considered a veteran crew, we took this new crew under our wing. I spoke to the flight engineer and told him he would do just fine. I gave him several tips that would help him and his crew on their first mission. I did not tell him what a difficult target Merseburg would be, for they would find that out soon enough. It would be my crew's third run over Merseburg, and to us, it was getting to be old hat. I felt, as did many crews, that it was just as difficult a target as Berlin, and, as we expected, the anti-aircraft fire could not have been any worse. The Germans must have had hundreds of batteries of 88-millimeter gunners ringing the city. What made it even worse was the fact that we were going in at lower altitudes than we had the previous two times. While it may have been easier to hit our target at these lower altitudes, it also gave the anti-aircraft gunners a better chance of shooting us down. One thing in our favor, however, was that this time we

The Lady From Hell

would have fighter escorts with us all the way into and out of the city.

This is me in front of a P-47 Thunderbolt, also a favorite escort of mine.

    During the bomb run, I saw the new crew get hit by flak. They were flying off our right wing, and I saw it all. They were hit right under the number three engine. It sheared the wing off, and the plane went into a spin. It was their first mission, and they never had a chance. The centrifugal force from the spin prevented them from bailing out, and they vanished into the black sky below. They never even got to release their bombs. I had an eerie feeling about this, as it could have easily happened to us. It happened not more than one hundred feet from where we were. I thought to myself, "God, have mercy on them and comfort their loved ones when they receive that dreaded telegram informing them of the terrible news."

Despite this unfortunate incident, we hit the target well. We took out the ball bearing plants, and, needless to say, the plants at Schweinfurt and Merseburg would not be producing ball bearings for a long time. Ironically, we later found out that Germany had stock piled enough ball bearings to last over two years. Even if they had depleted their supply after this, they could import all the ball bearings they needed from Sweden, a neutral country that also manufactured them. We lost

The Lady From Hell

all those men, and all those planes, and we accomplished nothing. Some of the other groups involved in this raid hit the oil refineries in Merseburg, inflicting heavy damage. The Germans seemed to concentrate their defense on critical landmarks such as these oil refineries and military manufacturing plants. One of the aircraft manufacturing plants, I.G. Farben, was extremely well defended, but despite this, it was badly damaged during this raid.

As we flew past the tower, where they counted the number of returning planes, my thoughts turned to the new crew that would not return from their first mission. I was again aware of how lucky we were to return from this, or any, mission. Once again, when we arrived back at our barracks, we saw six empty bunks.

I got sick that night. Maybe it was the food at dinner, or maybe I ate too fast, or maybe just staring at six empty bunks got to me this time. I was sick several times that night, and the next day I felt as if I had been hit by a truck. God, how I wished this war would end!

17

EUROPE'S WINTER WEATHER

Missions eleven through fifteen were over the cities of Stuttgart, Kassel, Bullay, Magdeburg, and Cologne. We were now one of the senior crews, and during most of our missions we flew as one of the lead planes in the formation. The format was always the same. Bomb the hell out of the target, get out of the flak area as quickly as possible, and get back to base safely. If you were lucky, you could do this again on another day.

The winter weather in Europe was becoming a big problem. Either the fog was so thick in England, or the target was "weathered in." The words, "takeoff delayed because of weather" could be mighty frustrating. A joke that was circulating through the 305th Bomb Group said it all. The tower asked the pilot, "Can you see the runway lights?" The pilot replied, "#@%#, I can't even see my co-pilot!"

You smoked a lot more than you should have while you waited, and waited, and waited some more. Finally, the word came to get ready for take off. On one mission, the weather over the target area was clearing, but unfortunately the fog at Chelveston had not. In fact, it was so thick, that not only couldn't we see the runways from inside the cockpit, we could not see engines #1 or #4. The engines on the B-17 Flying Fortress were numbered from left to right from the standpoint of the cockpit, and the #1 and #4 engines were the outermost engines. Finally, after waiting for what seemed like forever, a jeep showed up with huge flares, and because we were unable to see anything, we had to follow him to the runway. We positioned ourselves at what we hoped was the end of the runway. This positioning was of the utmost importance during these winter days since we were carrying twelve five-hundred pound bombs, a full fuel load, thirteen fifty-caliber machine

The Lady From Hell

guns, loads of ammunition, and ten very concerned crewmembers. We certainly needed to use the entire runway to take off.

With the parking breaks set, we read the checklist, following every order as it was written. The pilot revved the engines to full throttle and released the breaks. "The Lady From Hell" lurched forward, and we headed down the runway. It was such an eerie feeling not to be able to see anything. We put our faith in God, and in the "Lady." When we reached a ground speed of one hundred and ten miles per hour, the pilot started to pull back on the yoke. At times, the air was so still we needed the help of the flaps to give the plane a lift. As soon as we were airborne, the landing gear came up, reducing the drag on the plane and enabling us to climb more quickly. After several minutes of flying blind, we finally broke out into the sunlight. It was the most beautiful sight; too many planes to count, all trying to locate their formations, so they could start out on the mission. We found our formation very quickly since we had become very proficient at this routine task. Our biggest concern was avoiding other planes that were looking for their formations simultaneously.

Since our takeoff had been delayed, we missed our escort. We would proceed to the target without those beautiful P-51s flying with us. I had a sick feeling that we might have missed them. The Luftwaffe took advantage of this, as they hit our formations time and time again. It never ceased to amaze me that as soon as the P-51s showed up, the Luftwaffe disappeared. The flak over the target was always bad. The 88-millimeter anti-aircraft guns that were used by the Germans were undoubtedly the best in the business, and we feared them tremendously. As I've said, I would rather face enemy fighters because at least you could shoot back at them. There was no defense against anti-aircraft fire. Unfortunately, the combination of a big bomb load and strong head winds made the big bombers inviting targets. Most of

The Lady From Hell

the time we hit our targets, but the price we paid was always high.

Weather was not only a problem during takeoff, but also upon returning from a mission. Sometimes formations would take longer to establish. Sometimes it became necessary to take evasive action, resulting in a longer route to the target. Sometimes we were bucking headwinds that were a lot stronger than the weather officer had forecast at the morning briefing. All of this affected our fuel consumption. The rule of thumb was that you would use two thirds of your fuel getting to the target, and one third of your fuel getting back to base after the bombs had been dropped. England was our biggest problem when returning from a mission. Many times it was either very overcast or very foggy. At times, visibility was so bad, we could not remain in formation, and we would get the word to break formation. We would then be on our own. This order caused a lot of near misses, and, as I've said before, there were too many times when two airplanes did not miss hitting each other.

      I remember one mission in particular when, after breaking formation, we became lost and could not find our airfield. We kept flying for a while, but with no luck. We were running very low on fuel, and, in fact, the fuel tank on engine #2 had run dry and the engine had stopped. I could not transfer fuel because the other three tanks were also running close to empty as well. The radio was of no help either, because we were unable to contact anyone. Perhaps it was because so many airplanes were seeking help that the airways were jammed, or because bad weather was causing problems. We would never know why, only that we were receiving a lot of static. Finally, through a small hole in the overcast, we spotted an airfield. We could see that the runways were not as long as we would have liked them to be, but at least they were there. While we were making our approach, we finally made radio contact with the tower, and informed them we had no choice but

The Lady From Hell

to land since we were running low on fuel. The reply from the tower was garbled, so we interpreted this as a clearance to land. The pilot landed the "Lady" as close to the edge of the runway as possible. It was an excellent landing, and as soon as the wheels touched the runway, he applied the breaks. Because of his skill, we were able to stop before running off the end of the runway and into a big ditch. Afterwards, while taxiing the plane towards the hangar, the #3 engine ran out of fuel, and it stopped. The other two engines must have been running on fumes.

This airfield belonged to an English fighter group. I don't believe that I have ever met a nicer group of people in my life. They called our airfield in Chelveston to advise them that we had landed safely. I was not surprised when we heard only two airplanes had made it back to base. Like us, all the rest had landed in airfields all over England. The English crewmembers then invited us to have dinner at the officers' mess hall, and we had a beautiful, very English-like dinner, complete with tea and biscuits. After dinner, they took us to their version of our P.X., where we drank and exchanged war stories. I was very surprised to hear about how much they admired our B-17 Flying Fortresses. They were equally impressed that we bombed our German targets during the day. The English bombers bombed only at night. We gave a tour of the Flying Fortress to those who wanted one. I think everyone based in the airfield went through our plane. They could not believe that we carried thirteen fifty-caliber machine guns. They had heard many stories on how some B-17s returned to base even though they were very badly damaged. The English were a fantastic group of people, both heroic and proud, and rightfully so. I, for one, was very happy that they were our allies.

After refueling, we headed back to Chelveston. When we returned, we received two news bulletins, one good, the other, not so good. The bad news was that we were now required to fly thirty missions,

The Lady From Hell

instead of twenty-five. The raids over Berlin, Schweinfurt, Leipzig, Merseburg, and other cities, were taking their toll on us. We were promised that the P-51 fighter escorts would now accompany all future missions. This made the bad news a little easier to take. The other news was a lot nicer. We were going to a home for some much needed rest and relaxation for two weeks. The home was located just outside of London, and was previously owned by some Prime Minister. We would take a train to London, and a mini-bus would pick us up and take us to our new home. I, for one, was certainly looking forward to the next two weeks.

Our new home was something else. It was more like a castle than a home. Whoever owned this home certainly knew how to live. We each had our own room, mine with a huge canopy over the bed. I had seen things like this in the movies, but never in real life. It would be something to write home about, and it only got better. If we wanted, we could have breakfast in bed, served between the hours of 0700 and 0800. Lunch and dinner were served in the main dining room. Lunch would be served between 1200 and 1300 hours, while dinner would be served between 1900 and 2000 hours. In between, there were all kinds of snacks available to us. Three crews of enlisted men, totaling eighteen, were housed and serviced at one time. The officers were sent to a different rest home. We were from three different groups, but we flew many of the same missions. We got along extremely well, as if we had known each other for years. We all had the same fears, and we all shared the same wish; that the war would end soon so we could all go home. But above all, we were American war buddies, and that made us brothers.

The Lady From Hell

Two weeks of rest and relaxation was ordered for our crew. It was something we desperately needed. Here I'm rafting on a lake outside of London.

There were numerous things to do at our new home. We could go horseback riding, play golf, or go fishing in the huge lake located right on the grounds. Weather permitting, we could go on a picnic, or we could even visit London. If we were seeking peace and quiet, we could stay at the home, sink into one of those big leather chairs in front of a roaring fireplace, and read the papers while sipping a brandy. I spent several days doing just that, catching up on the news from home. They had several papers from the United States, including the New York Times, and even though the papers were about a week old, it was good to read about what was happening at home. During this time, I did it all. I went horseback riding twice. It was the first time I had ever been on a horse, and although I had a sore bottom, it was worth the pain. I even played golf and impressed the pro assigned to the group. I hit some good long drives, and they went straight ahead. Golf was also a first for me.

    I took some long walks into the wooded areas located around the property, just to be by myself. It would allow me to think about things not related to the war, something I desperately needed to do. I thought about being a kid again, when I was in Brooklyn playing ball in the streets, and playing hockey on roller skates. God, how far away Brooklyn seemed. It seemed like a world away. Would I ever see it again? Would there be a mission from which I would not return? If the war would end right now,

The Lady From Hell

it would be a different Brooklyn to which I would be returning. In the late twenties and early thirties, when I was a little boy, life was much different. In the early forties, Brooklyn had become a metropolis, with more cars and trucks than I could have ever imagined. Regardless, this was still "my" Brooklyn, and I would have given anything to be there.

    I also took several trips to London. I saw two movies and a play. I did some shopping and just browsed around. The people of London had seen a lot of the war, maybe too much. The continuous bombings by the Luftwaffe had caused considerable damage, yet they went on as if nothing had happened. The English people were amazing and, as I have said before, I'm glad they were on our side. To tell the truth, I could have easily gotten used to living like this. However, all good things must come to an end. The two weeks went by so fast, I could not believe it. Whoever said that time flies when you're having fun, must have visited this home.

Frank J. Condreras

    The ride back to our base was a downer, as going back to war is never a fun situation. So far we had survived fifteen missions. Could our luck hold out for another fifteen? I was happy to see the same faces in our barracks when we arrived at the base. Our barracks had not lost any men while we were gone.

    The weather in England continued to be brutally cold. According to some newspapers, 1944 was the coldest European winter ever recorded in fifty years. The holiday season was now approaching.

    Christmas and New Year's were about a week away, but somehow the holiday spirit was not there. I got very emotional during this time of the year. I kept thinking about my family and Brooklyn. What would they be doing during the holidays? Did they have a nice Christmas tree? Were the presents under the tree? What would they be eating on each of the holidays? Would they be having company for the holidays? God, how I missed them. When I went to bed on Christmas Eve, for the first time in my

The Lady From Hell

adult life, I cried. I hid my face in my pillow, so no one could see or hear me. I tried to stop, but I couldn't. I cried myself to sleep that night. I woke up the next morning, and it was Christmas Day, 1944. There was no Christmas tree, and no presents, only the damn war.

During the holidays, the Allies and Germany agreed on a "Cease-fire" order which would last through New Years' Day. Both sides kept their word, and no shots were fired. However, at 0001 hours on January 2, 1945, artillery shells began exploding on both sides, and the war continued...

18

THE DESTRUCTION CONTINUES

Missions sixteen through twenty-six continued to rain destruction on the German war machine. Although the power of the Luftwaffe had been reduced significantly, they still managed to inflict some damage to the big bombers. A mission's danger and difficulty was usually measured by how long we were over enemy territory. We also wondered, would we meet our escorts on time? Would the Luftwaffe be active? How heavy would the anti-aircraft fire be? With the Allies advancing on all fronts, we would be spending less and less time over enemy territory, and that was definitely a good thing.

Some of the cities we hit were Koblenz, Mannheim, Berlin, Dortmund, Nurnberg, Munich, Bremen, and Swinemunde, among others, and not necessarily in this order. Before the end of my missions, my crew would have bombed the city of Berlin on three occasions and made it back safely every time. Unfortunately, not many crews could boast of this accomplishment. Our targets included oil refineries, oil storage depots, hydroelectric plants, railroad yards, manufacturing plants, submarine pens, and shipyards. All these targets were crucial to the German military operation.

The weather continued to be a problem during our missions. It seemed to follow a pattern. When it was foggy or we had ice and snow in England, the target was clear. Conversely, when it was clear in England, the target was "socked in" and visibility was poor. In these cases, we would wind up bombing the secondary or tertiary targets. Because of such last minute target changes, our escorts were often late, or would fail to show up at all. Despite this, the Luftwaffe did not cause us the problems they once did. It seemed that even though we were sometimes without escorts, the fear that the P-51s might be lurking in the vicinity was enough to cause the Luftwaffe to curtail its activities. However, when big industrial cities were the targets, the Luftwaffe would throw whatever planes they could against the formations. So dominant were we in the air that General Eisenhower advised all his ground troops that if they saw an airplane in the sky, it belonged to the Allies. Our dominance was undeniable, even to the Germans.

There would be times when the Luftwaffe did not show at all. On such occasions, the leader of the escort group would break radio silence and contact the German command on the ground, challenging them to come up and fight. Even though we knew they got the message, there was no response. A joke that was circulating at that time was that a German general at the front lines was telling his troops that if they saw planes in the sky, they were either Royal Air Force or U.S. Air Force, depending if they were blue or silver. He further concluded that if they saw no airplanes in the sky, then they belonged to the Luftwaffe!

The P-51s had become our favorite escort. They could fly with us all the way into Germany, wait for us while we bombed our targets, and then escort us home, paying special attention to the bombers that were damaged during the bomb run by flak. Damaged bombers would have difficulty keeping up with the formation and they needed extra protection. Just a month earlier, these airplanes would have been easy prey for the Luftwaffe. On one of these missions, the "Lady" was hit several times while on the bomb run, causing us to lose an engine and our oxygen system. We had already dropped our bombs, and we were at an altitude of about twenty-five thousand feet. It became necessary to dive down to a safe altitude, where we could breathe without the aid of oxygen. So down and down we went, reaching air speeds in excess of two hundred fifty miles per hour, despite operating with only three engines. The "Lady" shook and vibrated, making for a nervous time. Gradually, the pilot pulled back on the yoke, and we leveled out at about ten thousand feet, much to the relief of the crew. Once again, the "Lady" had come through for us.

It was about this time that we spotted two fighters coming at us. At that distance, it was impossible to know whether they were American or German fighters. The P-51s and the Messerschmidts were similar in appearance. In gunnery school, we were taught that a fighter could only harm us if their noses were pointed at our plane. The German Air Force had been using American markings on their planes, in an attempt to fool the bomber crews, but regardless of the markings, whether German or American, if they pointed their noses at us, we would fire immediately. An American fighter pilot would never point the nose of his plane at a bomber. Needless to say, we were greatly relieved when two beautiful P-51s slid up along side of us, like two guardian angels. I felt like walking out on the wing and giving them both a big hug. They broke radio silence and asked if we were okay. They had seen us dive out of the formation, and, seeing we were in trouble, decided to follow us, for which we were most grateful. It is because of them, and other pilots like them, that I am here to write my story. Those two P-51s stayed with us until we were out of enemy territory. Then, and only then, did they bid us good luck, and disappeared into the distance.

Although the weather continued to play a tremendous part in our operations, our biggest enemy continued to be the heavy flak we encountered around each city we would bomb. On one mission, the Eighth Air Force sent up some three hundred bombers in a raid on a German city. On this mission, the 305th Bomb Group contributed thirty-six planes. None of the planes were attacked directly by enemy fighters, but the flak was so heavy, that twenty of the thirty-six bombers returned to base with heavy battle damage. "The Lady From Hell" was one of the twenty seriously damaged. After we landed, we counted over one hundred holes in our plane. At least we had come back, and we had all four engines running.

The Lady From Hell

We had been coming back with only three engines so often that John Gunn, our ground-crew chief, remarked that he did not recognize the airplane with all four engines running!

The raid on the city of Dresden caused complete devastation. We had heard via the rumor mill that the bombing of Dresden was planned by the head of the Royal Air Force. He was incensed at the Luftwaffe's bombings of London and other large cities in England, and he claimed that it was the intention of the Germans to kill civilians rather than military personnel. The bombings of London, both day and night, had caused many deaths and tremendous destruction to the city. It was said that he vowed that someday, he would get his revenge. Since the Allies were now the ones doing the bombing, there would be no better target than the under-defended, over-populated city of Dresden.

Dresden was a city that had very little military value. It was possibly this reason that the German people believed the city would be safe from Allied bombings. The Germans, trying to avoid the Russian advances in the east and the Allied advances in the west, streamed into the already over-populated city of Dresden. It was payback time.

The Royal Air Force hit the city at night, with tons of incendiaries, which are bombs that start huge fires that erupt into fire storms. The Eighth Air Force was not entirely removed from this attack. During the days that followed the initial raid, the B-17s dropped tons of bombs on the burning city of Dresden. The fire storm raged uncontrollably for many days. It could be seen over hundreds and hundreds of miles. The death toll was staggering, measuring in the hundreds of thousands. People in shelters were burned alive. The fire was so huge, and consumed so much oxygen, that people were unable to breath, and suffocated to death. The bombs that were dropped did not discriminate. They killed everyone in their path, including the elderly, children, babies, cats, and dogs. What

The Lady From Hell

had we become? Even animals didn't kill indiscriminately, only to feed themselves. Maybe we, the human race, were the real animals. What cause is worth such destruction and mass murder?

Many German cities lay in ruins after multiple bomb runs.

Although Dresden was generally considered to be the most destructive raid in the European war, there were others just as bad. Unfortunately, I participated in several Berlin raids that involved over one thousand bombers. These missions required a maximum effort from all groups. It was hard to conceive how anyone could survive these horrible bombings. At the time, no figures were released regarding the number of deaths. Maybe it was just as well.

The city of Leipzig was hit even harder, again with over one thousand bombers. The destruction was beyond description. It just went on and on, one city after another, and "The Lady From Hell" participated in these raids. I am not bragging, nor am I proud of these situations. Our rationalization, at the time, was that the German nation was now going through the pain and suffering they had inflicted on the rest of the world not too long ago. War is not very pretty. I once read that the definition of war was pain, suffering, death, and destruction, but not necessarily in that order.

On another raid, the Army requested that the Eighth Air Force knock out a bridge on the Rhine River. It had become a sore spot. Rumor had it that several bombing runs over this target had been unsuccessful. Apparently, the Germans were using the bridge to move supplies, severely hampering an American infantry division close to the bridge in the process. It was thought that

The Lady From Hell

the previous missions had failed because the bombers had dropped their bombs from too high an altitude. This time we would go in at a much lower altitude. The risks would be greater, but the accuracy would improve tremendously. The 305th Bomb Group was assigned to take out this bridge, and we completed the task. The bridge no longer existed after that raid, as it lay in rubble beneath the Rhine River. "The Lady From Hell" was one of the lead airplanes on this mission, and she did her usual splendid job. She lost an engine and sustained some body damage, but on three engines, we limped home. Some of my buddies were not so lucky. Flying at such low altitudes made for an inviting target, and, again, we paid the price. Still, in Army terms, the mission was considered a success, because we had achieved the intended result.

Despite the losses, it was a good feeling to know that we had helped out an American infantry division. No outfit could be more deserving. Several days later, recognizing our efforts, the 305th Bomb

Frank J. Condreras

Group received the Presidential Citation for a job well done.

19

FAREWELL TO A LADY

No one knew on the morning of March 17, 1945 that we would not be returning that day. It was St. Patrick's Day, and we had slept restlessly, as we always did the night before a mission. What we did not know was that, after that day, our lives would never be the same. This was to be our twenty-seventh mission, and it started out much the same way as the previous twenty-six. We were awakened between 0330 and 0400 hours in the morning, and we washed and waited for the trucks to arrive to take us to the mess hall. Although I was a little cranky from lack of sleep, and I was nervous and scared, I still ate a good breakfast. Some of my buddies were not so lucky, as nervous stomachs did not desire food, and if you forced it down, it might not stay there.

After breakfast, the trucks took us to

the briefing room, where we found out that we were to bomb manufacturing plants in a city called Jena. It was located on the Saale River and was the headquarters of the Zeiss Optical Firm. The Allies had suspected that the factories were involved in some kind of a secret war project. Jena is a small town, located near the city of Leipzig, not very far from the Polish and Czech borders which, at the time, were occupied by German troops. This would be a long mission, and we would spend many hours over enemy territory. According to the briefing officer, there would be nothing to worry about. There would be very little anti-aircraft fire, and our P-51 escorts would be with us most of the way. The briefing officer indicated that this mission would be a "milk run," which was easy enough for him to say since he was not participating in the mission. To those of us who were flying these missions, there was no such thing as a "milk run." I hated to hear those words. There were just too many things that could go wrong and cause major

The Lady From Hell

problems. From previous experiences, I didn't take everything the briefing officer said as gospel. I felt that sometimes he sugarcoated the truth to make the crews feel more comfortable. Maybe he just didn't have all the facts, or maybe the Germans wanted us to think it would be a "milk run." We were to hit the target at 27,000 feet, which was pretty high for a milk run. As for me, I felt the higher the altitude, the better. My thinking was that the higher you were, the more time you had to get out of the plane, should it get hit. Despite the predicted light anti-aircraft fire, one good hit could end the war for you.

So, on that morning, we boarded "The Lady From Hell" that had become like a second home to us. We left the base at 0900 hours, carrying an extra five-hundred pound bomb. As we broke out of the clouds, there were lots of Flying Fortresses looking for their formations. We found ours quite easily because we were a veteran crew, and we knew the drill well. As we approached Germany, we noticed our escorts. They were buzzing all around us, making sure that they did not point their noses at the formations. I also noticed that the formations flew a lot looser now. It was more relaxing to know that your buddy's wing was not going to hit your wing. We were able to fly this way because we knew that if the Luftwaffe came up to get us, they would have to go through the P-51s, and they had not been too successful in doing so. Still, as we approached our target, the formations started to get closer together.

We were now at our assigned altitude of 27,000 feet, and the temperature was fifty degrees below zero. We were on oxygen, and had been for quite a while. As we started on the bomb run, we experienced a runaway propeller on engine #2. A runaway propeller could cause a very dangerous situation. If you did not feather it quickly enough, the force could shear the propeller off its shaft and into the plane. There were stories that it could easily cut an airplane in two. We also had a bomb bay full of bombs that could explode. About a minute and

The Lady From Hell

several prayers later, we were able to feather the propeller, and had to shut the engine down, as we continued in formation.

We dropped our bombs on the target, which lightened our load significantly. We were in heavy flak, and the visibility was poor on this so-called "milk run." I heard a loud bang, as we took a hit on engine #3. Several pieces of shrapnel tore through the cabin, narrowly missing my legs, but leaving holes in the cabin walls. The engine was not quite so lucky. It caught fire immediately, and we shut it down as quickly as possible, but it did not stop the fire. I don't know of anything more frightening than being 27,000 feet in the air at temperatures of fifty degrees below zero, sucking on an oxygen tube to survive, with a fire spreading from the engine over a wing with hundreds of gallons of fuel. We closed the cowling, hoping to suffocate the fire from lack of oxygen, and we also fired the fire extinguishers in the engine's nacelle. This seemed to put the fire out, however, we were now leaving a trail of heavy black smoke behind, making us very visible and very vulnerable. So, with only two of our four engines running, we had a big decision to make. Should we try for Sweden, which was a neutral country, or should we try to reach the Russian lines in Poland? We knew that the Germans and the Russians were engaged in very heavy fighting in Poland, but we were not sure of the exact location.

    We decided by majority vote that we would head for the Russian lines, somewhere in Poland. We would head east for as long as the "Lady" would take us. As it was, we didn't have much choice, but again, luck was with us. The German Air Force never showed. Of course, as an alternative, we could have bailed out, but the fear of what the Germans would do to us if we were captured ruled that option out. To lighten the plane as much as possible, we threw out all our heavy equipment, including the entire ball turret assembly. We threw out all our guns and ammunition, and we prayed that "The Lady From Hell" would deliver

The Lady From Hell

us safely, as she had done so many times before.

We descended for about an hour, leaving a trail of black smoke behind us. Our altitude was about six thousand feet. The pilot had to keep the nose of the plane down, in a gradual descent, so as to keep the air speed up, otherwise we would go into a spin. That hour seemed endless. We listened to the drone of engines #1 and #4 and prayed they would hold out. When engine #4 started to overheat, we opened up the cowling as far as we could, and we cut the power in half. The "Lady" was now starting to vibrate, and it was quite apparent that she was struggling to keep us airborne. We all had our parachutes on, just in case we couldn't make it. Our hearts grew heavier and our fear deepened. We had to land soon. Our altitude was now less than four thousand feet. Again, God was with us. We spotted an airfield, whose runway had been bombed or blown up. The condition of the runway left us no choice but to land with our wheels up, on the belly of the plane. There was a muddy swamp next to the runway, and we hoped it would serve to cushion our inevitable crash landing. Whether we were in German or Russian territory made no difference. We had no choice but to land, and we hoped we weren't about to land on any bombs. As we approached the swampy area next to the runway, the plane began to shutter and shake, as I'd never seen her do before. We were ten very frightened crewmembers, praying for survival. Our fate was in the hands of God right now. If we were about to land in German territory, the possibility of being tortured by the Germans was unthinkable. If not, the thought of survival was almost as unthinkable. As the "Lady" hit the swampy ground below, the noise was unparalleled. I was thrown around and jostled as she tore through the muddy swamp. I heard and saw my fellow crewmembers get bumped around in their respective areas as we continued to come to an abrupt halt. I had been with my pilot in a hundred landings and takeoffs, but this

The Lady From Hell

landing was a true test of his skills. He came through for us with flying colors. As best he could, he made a picture perfect landing out of a horrible and traumatic situation. All the propellers were bent and the plane was buried in the muck of the swamp. The only thing that was visible was the top of the cockpit and the huge tail. The only way out of the airplane was through the top of the radio hatch.

Miraculously enough, the crew came out in pretty good shape, suffering some cuts, bumps, and bruises. We were very lucky, considering that the other side of the runway was littered with mines and unexploded bombs, left by the Germans in their hasty retreat. Had we landed there, we would have all been dead. Once again, "The Lady From Hell" had delivered us safely to the ground below. She had served us well, but now it was time to say goodbye. For me, this was not a very easy thing to do. I had spent so much time in this airplane that she had become a part of me. And so, on March 17, 1945, a part of me also died. That was the last time I ever saw her. She had a life span of less than two years, beginning in an aircraft factory in Seattle, Washington, and ending in the swamps of the Black Forests of Poland. During her time with us, she had served her country well, and on this day, she left behind a very grateful crew. So, it was with misty eyes, that I said goodbye and thank you to the greatest B-17 Flying Fortress in the Eighth Air Force. I will never forget "The Lady From Hell." Our "milk run" was now completed.

20

RESCUED BY THE RUSSIANS

Where were we? Were we in German or Russian hands? Did we get into Poland far enough to reach our allies? Our questions were answered very quickly as a group of Russian soldiers, fully armed, descended upon us. We learned we had crashed near a city called Radom, which was located some fifty miles south of the capital city of Warsaw, Poland. The place we crashed was called the Black Forest and, to this day, I don't know whether this was the actual name of the forest or a nickname given it because of the heavy fighting that occurred there. At this time, we were advised that we were prisoners of war, and were 'detained' in a cell until such time as our identities could be verified. If we were not identified within a certain time frame, we could be considered spies and enemies. It was indeed a very frightening situation, especially since wartime spies did not usually fare well. Reasoning with these people was impossible. First of all, there was the language barrier, and secondly, reasoning with front line Russian soldiers was like banging your head against a brick wall.

We were put into a jail cell, separate from the German prisoners, an act for which we were very grateful. I'm sure the German prisoners would know we were not German immediately. They were kept outside in the cold, behind barbed wire fences. There were thousands of them there.

Our surroundings reminded me of a jail scene commonly seen in a western movie. There would always be a guard on duty watching us. There would be a guard change every four hours. Several times a day, we would be interrogated by what we felt was the Russian KGB, which was the equivalent of our FBI or CIA. All in all, we were treated fairly well.

Food, or lack of food, was a problem. In the mornings we were given a thick slice

The Lady From Hell

of black bread and a cup of very watery tea. There was a soft spread, otherwise known as butter, which we could spread on this black bread. Actually, it was lard, not butter. At night we again received a slice of this black bread, along with a cup of watery soup which contained potato skins and cabbage. The guard would tell us there was meat in the soup, however no one ever found anything that resembled meat in their soup. Incidentally, the menu never changed.

In the morning, after breakfast, a truck would pick us up and take us to a farm, where we picked cabbage, potatoes, and other cold-weather vegetables. I looked forward to the truck ride and the farming. It made the day go by much faster, relieving the boredom. We were detained in these cells for over a week before word came through from our headquarters and our American identities were finally confirmed.

After our release from prison, even our guards hugged us and offered us parts of their rations. We were visited by a Russian officer, who advised us that a good dinner was being prepared for us. He told us that we would eat this dinner in the officers' mess hall. It was indeed a beautiful dinner, including some good cuts of meat. He apologized for keeping us in prison and told us he had suspected all along that we were really American, and allies of Russia. But during a war, you could not take any chances. He told us that the Germans were using captured B-17s to bomb Russian positions. We were not aware of this. He also warned us that, although the majority of the Black Forest was under Russian control, there were isolated pockets of Germans that had been overrun in the Russian advance and were still holding out. We learned from him that we would be sent to the Russian city of Poltava, which was located not far from the Black Sea. It was where all Allied personnel were sent. We would wait in Poltava, and when transportation became available, we would be returned to our base in England,

The Lady From Hell

avoiding the active war areas in Europe during our journey back.

The following day, the Russians advised us that there would be a freight train leaving Radom and heading east in the very near future. The boxcars would be full of Polish refugees hoping to get back home. We would ride on top of the freight, along with the Russian soldiers. The soldiers would be armed, in case we encountered any German resistance while riding through the Black Forest. We were also given guns and told to follow instructions from the sergeant in charge, should anything happen.

The guns they gave us were United States carbine rifles. Ironically, these were the same guns with which we had trained in basic training. At least we were familiar with the weapons we were given. It also appeared to us that they were expecting trouble. I had never ridden in a freight train before, much less on top of one, so this was a first for me, as well as for my entire crew. The next morning, the train pulled out slowly and cautiously because of potential mines. A jeep with mine detectors rode in front of the train, proceeding very cautiously. We had been riding for about two hours, when suddenly, we heard machine guns fire. All at once, the train came to a complete stop. Russian soldiers jumped off of the train and ran into the forest, firing their machine guns as they ran. The sergeant in charge of us also jumped off the train and motioned us to do the same. We followed as the gunfire intensified. We heard some big explosion. The Russian sergeant informed us, in his broken English, that it was Russian artillery at work, and we were told to crawl on our bellies, and get as low to the ground as possible. I had not been trained for this kind of fighting. Ground warfare was a new experience for me, and I was very frightened. It was just too close for comfort. After twenty-seven successful air missions, I thought about the irony of dying while fighting with the Russians against the German army in a forest in Poland. The war department would have

The Lady From Hell

a hard time selling that to my parents. My thoughts were interrupted when I heard loud, clanging noises. Just as the sergeant had said, Russian tanks came rolling past us, knocking down trees as they went. There were many Russian soldiers running behind these tanks, rifles in hand, ready to fight the enemy. The sergeant told us to stay where we were, on our bellies, and it would all be over shortly.

Sure enough, as quickly as the gunfire had started, it stopped. The sergeant's information was very accurate. Russian soldiers began returning, laughing and smoking cigarettes. They shared these cigarettes with us in celebration. There were no German prisoners taken at this time. These attacks were initiated by pockets of German soldiers, who were isolated by the rapid Russian advances weeks earlier. They were trying to get back to their outfits.

When we got back to the tracks, the train that I thought would be waiting for us was long gone.

Frank J. Condreras

This is part of my crew with Russian officers and civilian interpreters. This picture was taken somewhere in Poland.

The Russians took us to the headquarters of the Russian Gestapo. We were given a room and strict orders not to go out at night, or anytime without the guards and the interpreter. I suppose we were under constant observation, or at least that was the impression we got. In our room there was both a bathtub and

The Lady From Hell

hot water. We were given soap and a towel, so we bathed. We were given clean underwear made out of flour sack material, but at least it was clean. After bathing, they sent a barber to shave us and give us haircuts. We were then introduced to the colonel who headed this outfit. He asked us a lot of questions and informed us we would be his guests for the next day or so. Near the end of March, out of a clear blue sky, we were awakened at 0400 hours in the morning. We were given ten loaves of bread that seemed to weigh one hundred pounds, nine cans of fat meat, one pound of lard, three pounds of sugar and some tea. These rations were meant to last five days. A Russian lieutenant, an interpreter, and two soldiers with machine guns were to accompany us to Lotz, Poland. We had definite orders to proceed, but no idea how long this journey would take. We were advised to proceed by the best route we could find. The soldiers and personnel accompanying us were there to assist us.

We started off by riding in a railroad

work car, and then changed to a boxcar, in which we rode for twenty-four hours. In the daylight hours, we rode on top of the cars. It felt good to breathe the fresh air, and it also gave the Polish women and children more room inside the car. Besides, the weather was nice and there was no threat of any German resistance, since we were now a long way from the Black Forest. The next night we slept in a railroad station which was bombed out. We started off the next day on foot; then changed to a horse-drawn carriage which was commandeered by the Russian lieutenant in charge of us. Finally, we found ourselves back on a railroad car, full of coal, which took us into Lotz. We slept in the railroad station that night, and finally, at about 1000 hours the next morning we rode through the town in a streetcar. Streetcars had just begun to run again after the Germans had left.

At Lotz, we found some Americans and learned that our destination was an airfield about thirty miles north of Lotz, near Palo, Poland. We arrived near the airfield

The Lady From Hell

that night by cattle car, and, after arriving, we were turned over to the town's people as guests for the night. Here we met some of the nicest people you could ever meet. The family with whom I stayed consisted of an elderly mother, two daughters, and two granddaughters. They treated me like I was a god. They had a nice home in comparison to some of the others I had seen. They also had a Polish-English dictionary so we were able to carry on quite a conversation. They really believed that America was the only country in which to live, and that only the United States could save the world. Nearly everyone to whom I spoke had relatives in America. This family had relatives in Chicago, and knowing I was from New York, they thought I might know them. I explained to them that there were over fifteen million people between the two cities, and that I did not know their relatives.

Breakfast consisted of a slice of that famous black bread and egg that had been scrambled and fried, and then spread on the bread. It tasted great. When you're hungry, everything tastes great. What amazed me was that the black bread, no matter how old, always appeared fresh, even thought it could be a week old. I think their secret was that they kept it wrapped tightly in a damp cloth. After breakfast they took me back to the town square where I met the rest of my crew. They also enjoyed the same hospitality as I had. Before I left for the town square I had written a note, with the help of the Polish-English dictionary, thanking them for everything they did for me. I left my name and address in America, should they ever come to the United States. I also left whatever money I had, since they were so poor. When I told the Russian lieutenant, he laughed and said that we Americans were too soft. Be that as it may, the fact remained that the Polish people were very warm and generous. I must also say that the Russian people with whom I came in contact were also warm and generous, despite being in such a horrible war for such a long period of time. After all, it was the Russians who

The Lady From Hell

saved us, and were trying to get us back to our base safely. I can't begin to think of the torturous treatment the Germans would have dished out to us if they had been our captors.

The airfield was about three miles from the town square, although, when you were walking, it felt like a lot more than that. When we arrived at the airfield, we found another B-17 crew that had been shot down over Berlin the day after we had been shot down. The crew was also from the 305th Bomb Group, making it feel like old home week. Their crew had to bail out, and two of them were captured by the Germans. The navigator broke his leg in the jump. We also met a P-51 pilot, who was shot down in a dogfight. He was from Brooklyn. He and I shared a common emotion; we both missed Brooklyn tremendously. We were to wait at the airfield until a plane showed up. If no plane showed we were to walk back to the town square and repeat the same process again tomorrow. Unfortunately, no plane showed up either that day or the next day.

The third day, a C-47 flew in by accident, and it flew us all to Poltava, Russia. We left our Russian escort at the airfield in Palo, Poland. We arrived just in time, for the following day no one was allowed to take off anywhere in Russia except for Russian pilots.

When we got to Poltava, Russia, we were at last in American hands, however, very much under the Russian jurisdiction. We were interned here almost three weeks. We were allowed to go into the city, but only at the times specified by the Russian command. There was nothing much to do in the city of Poltava, but it was different than being on the base. These were civilian people with whom we were able to mingle. I even enjoyed the Russian food. I was impressed at how well the Russian people treated us. It was here that we received the news that President Roosevelt had died. It amazed me how many Russians shared our grief. All flags were flown at half-mast, and most businesses were closed. I wished that he could have been

The Lady From Hell

around to see the German and Japanese empires fall. He had suffered through a long and hard war. Many times, especially during the early years of the war, the news was very depressing, yet it was his job to convince the American public that, in the end, victory would be ours. Many times, it was a hard sell. God bless you, President Roosevelt, and peace be with you.

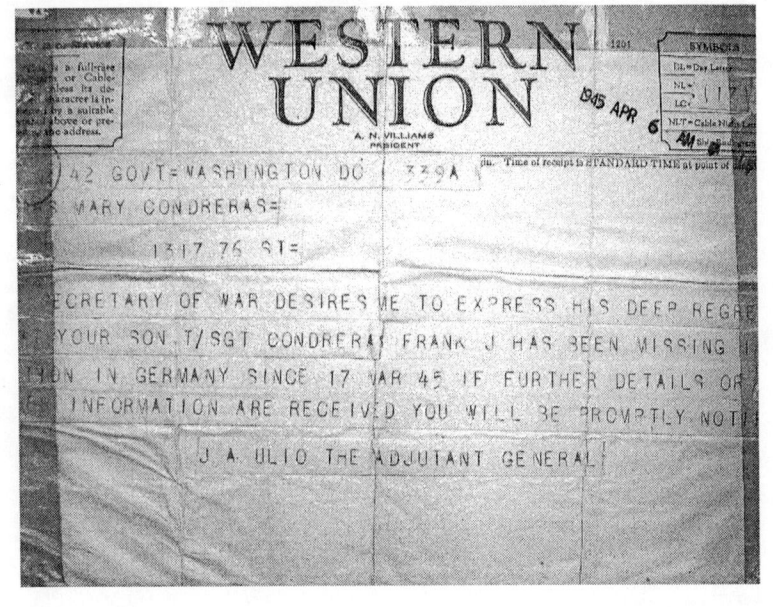

This was the dreaded telegram advising my family of my fate after being shot down on March 17, 1945.

Frank J. Condreras

One thing that bothered every one of us was the fact that there was practically no postal service. All of us had written home many times, and were promised that the letters would be delivered. We realized that our parents had received the infamous telegram that started out: The War Department regrets to inform you that your son, Technical Sergeant, Frank J. Condreras, had been missing in action since a raid over Germany on March 17, 1945. The format was always the same, but the names were different. We were hoping that one of the many letters we wrote would get through to our loved ones who were most certainly frantic with worry. In each letter we would ask who ever got a letter to notify the families of the rest of the crew. Although the Russians would not allow any telephone calls to the United States, they did guarantee that the letters we wrote would reach their destination eventually. We were, of course, reminded that all letters would be censored. Personally, I did not believe

The Lady From Hell

that any letters we wrote would ever reach the United States.

The time I spent traveling from Radom to Poltava was an experience that will stay with me the rest of my life. I will never forget the nights that we spent in the homes of the generous Polish and Russian families who were delighted to give us what little they had. The war had caused mass destruction. They were wonderfully warm, and these families made a very anxious and uncertain time much more bearable for us. I will never forget their generosity.

On another occasion, we were walking through Poland when we saw a long line of German prisoners being marched to a detaining area. This line went on and on endlessly. Many of these men were wounded and had dirty bandages in desperate need of changing. Fresh blood was still oozing through, and some were on make-shift crutches struggling to keep up with the formation. Many times, two of the prisoners would be carrying a third, half dragging him as they moved forward. It was a sad sight to see. One of the guards was brutally hitting them with the butt of his rifle, knocking them down, and causing more injuries. We went to the officer in charge and told him what we had seen. We advised him that the Geneva Convention states that all prisoners should be treated humanely. The officer's expression changed, and he said, "I must tell a little story about that sergeant."

He knew him personally, and very well. The sergeant's mother and father were killed by German storm troopers for no reason other than their Russian nationality. His wife and daughter were raped in front of one another by six German infantry men. After they were raped they were tied up in their own home and their home was set on fire, killing both of them. "You will have to explain the Geneva Convention to him, because I would not know where to start," said the officer.

War is horrible. It makes animals out of many men.

21

THE LONG TRIP BACK TO BASE

Towards the end of April, we were advised by the Russian captain in charge of transportation that we would be going back to our base. How long it would take depended on the availability of planes and pilots. The first leg of our journey would begin the next day at 1300 hours, and we would be going from Poltava to the city of Tehran, Persia, which is known today as Iran. Once there, we would wait for available transportation for the next leg of our journey. In the past, flying never bothered me. I had spent almost 1500 hours in the Flying Fortresses and loved every minute of it, but flying on the C-47 scared me. One thing I noticed, that I did not like, was all the oil on the wings, which indicated leaks somewhere along the line. Another thing that bothered me was that while flying through the mountain passes, when

Frank J. Condreras

I looked out the window, the mountains were higher than us on both sides of the plane. The last thing that bothered me was that the plane had only two engines and no parachutes. It was primarily a cargo plane and not equipped for passengers. What a difference from my Flying Fortress, which had four engines, parachutes for everyone, and flew high over the mountains rather than between them. So I felt great relief when I heard the wheels touch down at the Tehran airport.

There was an army truck there to meet us and take us to an American camp, right in the heart of Tehran. I never knew the U.S. maintained an army camp in Tehran. Let's face it, at that time, I had never heard of Tehran! The camp was there for the purpose of getting any American military men who had been shot down or had escaped from German prisoner of war camps back to their original bases. The camp was run in military fashion. The only entrance to the camp was patrolled by Military Police night and day. We would be allowed to

The Lady From Hell

visit the city, but we were cautioned to go in groups of three or four. We were also told that certain parts of the city were off limits, and not to get involved with any of the local women. Since we were only in Tehran for two days I did not get to see or do very much, but everywhere I turned I was reminded that there was a war going on.

We were advised that another plane would be waiting for us the next day. This plane would take us to Cairo, Egypt. It was very much the same as the first C-47, however, this time we did not have to climb very high or fly amidst mountains. Cairo was like a vacation. The first thing I liked was the warm weather. It seemed like the first time I felt warm since we had left England. The base where we stayed consisted of many tents. In fact, it reminded me of Tent City, where I received my basic training so long ago. Again, as in Tehran, the camp was run in military fashion. I didn't mind getting up early in the morning. No one was waking us up to go on a mission, and the war seemed a long way off now. Instead, we were getting up to go to the mess hall to have breakfast.

Our tent was not far from the Sphinx.

The personnel at the base told us that crews usually spent anywhere from two days to one week there, before leaving

The Lady From Hell

for their next destination. The camp was located right on the desert floor. When I stepped out of my tent, I could see the Sphinx and several pyramids. We did a lot while in Cairo. We went on a tour of the Sphinx and visited several pyramids. It was amazing to tour these structures. What was more amazing was the fact that they were built without any machinery. Stones that weighed tons were placed on top of one another. Truly, they were a marvel to behold. I also took a camel ride, which was very different from horseback riding. On a camel, you always feel like you're going to fall off.

Cairo was like a rest camp for us. I spent six of the most beautiful days of my life there. It was just what our crew needed after being shot down and held prisoners; a lot of rest and relaxation. The weather was warm, our living quarters were very comfortable, the food was good, and the army personnel treated us like royalty. All the questions we asked were answered with patience. We could get anything we needed and our time was our own. We could do anything or go anywhere we wanted, as long as we were available when our transportation arrived. It was here, in Cairo, that we were finally able to telephone our families, thanks to the army personnel in charge of communications.

While in Cairo, we were housed in a tent on the desert floor. Ours is in the background.

When I called home, my brother Ernie answered the phone, and with cracking voices, we greeted each other. Yes, they had received the telegram that indicated we were missing in action over Germany, but they knew we were safe in Russian hands.

The Lady From Hell

Somehow, a letter I had written in Poland had been smuggled out of Poland, reached American hands, and was forwarded to the United States. Out of the hundreds of letters we wrote in Poland and Russia, this one was the only one that had gotten through. I had not said much in the letter, except that we were well, safe, and in Russian hands. In each of the hundreds of letters, my crew and I had written the names and telephone numbers of our entire crew, so that if anyone's letter did get through, that family could call the other families and hopefully put their minds at ease. My family had, indeed, called all the families of my crew. My brother said that every call resulted in a long crying period, but they were tears of joy, which made a big difference. My brother further informed me that it was my father that came running into the house with my letter. He had not yet opened it, but he had met the postman en route to the house, which was an agreement the two had made.

This agreement was a result of the

Frank J. Condreras

fact that my mother was alone in the house the day the telegram from the war department arrived. When it was delivered, she was so happy to receive it, because she did not understand what it meant. The postman asked her why she was so happy. He then explained to her what receiving such a telegram from the war department meant. My mother screamed in anguished disbelief, and fainted to the ground. Being a diabetic, she must have gone into diabetic shock. My grandparents, who were home upstairs, came running down after hearing the commotion. Since that day, someone was always home with her to answer the door and the telephone, and the postman agreed to meet my father down the street. This way, if additional bad news came, at least it was the family who would break the news to her.

My brother told me that my father realized my letter was dated after the war department's telegram, so he concluded that, at least, I was alive. Mom was next door visiting a neighbor when I called, and

The Lady From Hell

someone had to go get her. When she got to the phone she was a little bit out of breath, and before she could say anything, she cried, which was her privilege. I cried because she cried. I assured her I was fine and that there was nothing wrong with me physically. Yes, the war, for me, was over. No, I would not fly any more combat missions. Yes, I should be coming home in the very near future. Yes, I'll take care of myself, and you do the same. I love you, and I love you too. I'll see you soon. Goodbye, mom.

My brother got on the phone again. He tried to describe how happy this phone call had made mom, but he couldn't. While I was talking to mom, he had gotten the telegram and insisted on reading it to me. Although I knew what the telegram said, I listened:

> The Secretary of war desires me to express his deep regret that your son T/Sgt. Condreras Frank J. has been missing in action over Germany since 17 March 1945. If further details or other information is received you will be promptly notified.

Frank J. Condreras

On our last day in Cairo we went into the city to do some shopping. We paid a lot more for what we bought than we should have. Maybe that Russian lieutenant was right. We Americans are too soft. When we returned from our shopping spree, we were told there would be an airplane landing in the morning that would be taking us to Athens, Greece. I was sorry to hear that in a way. I wouldn't have minded spending several more days in Cairo. Ever since my phone call home I was feeling great. My brother told me that the phone call was the best medicine my mother could have had, but it also worked wonders for me. Just knowing they were okay was a blessing, and it put my mind at peace. I noticed that same look on the faces of my fellow crewmembers. It was a look of satisfaction, happiness, and relief. I don't think anybody cared how long it would take us to get back to Chelveston anymore.

The Lady From Hell

The pyramids provided us with another beautiful view from our campground in Cairo.

The next day the plane arrived late because of mechanical problems. Although the plane's crew claimed the mechanical problems were fixed, I still had my concerns. How ironic, after surviving a war and twenty-seven air missions, to die while trying to get back to base. So, again, I worried until the wheels touched the runway at Athens. Upon landing we were met by four soldiers of the Greek army. The United States did not have a base in Athens. We were in the hands of the Greek army, and we stayed in a huge house, just off the airport. The building looked like it could have been a hotel before the war. One of the soldiers who spoke English informed us that we would be taken to dinner at 1800 hours, and to breakfast the next morning at 0800 hours. After that, we would be taken to the airport where a plane would meet us to take us to Naples, Italy. True to his word, at 1800 hours we were taken to a restaurant right in the city of Athens. They had a room set up for us in the back of the restaurant. We ate everything from soup to nuts, including some pretty good wine. Uncle Sam was paying some pretty big bucks to get us back to base. After dinner, we were taken back to our building. The good food and wine made us all feel pretty good, and we were indulging in some good conversation. We were laughing, joking, and telling war stories. It had been a long

The Lady From Hell

time since we had enjoyed ourselves. At this moment in time our problems seemed to be all behind us. We presumed that the war was over for us. From the reports we had heard from the English, Americans, and Russians along our journey, the Allies were ripping Germany apart. Everyone seemed to agree, it was only a matter of time before the end of the war.

The next morning, after breakfast, the Greek soldiers took us to the airport where there was a plane waiting for us. It was here that the Greek soldiers left us. We thanked them, and I must say, they were and are very proud and efficient people. The trip to Naples was uneventful, maybe because I was getting used to flying on the C-47. Upon our arrival, we were sent to a hotel right on the bay of Naples, in full view of Mt. Vesuvius. My mother was born in Naples, right near Mt. Vesuvius. How I would have loved to see the house she was born in, but I did not have the address. I sat down that night, after dinner, and wrote her a letter in which I stated that even though the war had hit Naples, it was still a very beautiful city. My buddies agreed that the bay of Naples, with Mt. Vesuvius in the background spewing fire from its top, was a marvelous sight. I was proud of my mother's birthplace, and, in my letter, I promised her that after the war ended we would return some day to Naples. I missed my mom, and I was sorry for all the grief that I had caused her; leaving her at eighteen years of age to go to war, being in combat, getting shot down, and that horrible telegram. Why did she have to go through all this? Why did any parent have to? Later on, after the war had ended, my sister, Yola, told me that the letter I sent from Poland was mom's favorite letter. She had saved it, and every once in a while, she would take it out and read it, and cry. I'm sorry, mom, for all the grief that I caused you.

We had spent several nice days in Naples. The weather was not as warm as it had been in Cairo, but it was comfortable. Since we were no longer in a hurry to get back, every day that the plane did not arrive was like a bonus. The Italian people were famous for their cooking, and we were not disappointed. We ate some good Italian food. It was as close to my mother's cooking as could be. Many restaurants were now open in Naples, as the war was over for these people. The Germans had long gone, and they were trying to return to their normal lives.

The rest of our trip back to base went by very quickly. We went from Naples to Paris, stopping only for an hour to refuel, and then took off for London. When we got to London, we were more or less on our own, and we decided unanimously to remain in London for a couple of days. Although we were anxious to get home to our families, we were not sure this would be the end of the war for us. We knew we might be required to fly more missions once we were back at our base, and we were not in a hurry to get back to that. We enjoyed whatever London had to offer. There were indeed a lot of changes going on at that time. Most of the rubble from the German bombings had been cleared, and there was even some minor construction going on. The English people never ceased to amaze me. It was almost as if they had never been in a war.

Finally, after two beautiful days in London, and with much regret, we took the train back to Chelveston. We were now on the final leg of our journey. There would be no army trucks to pick us up. Instead, we took cabs back to the base. We arrived on the evening of May 5th or 6th, I'm not exactly sure. It was nice to see our old buddies again, as we had so much to talk about. It had been seven long weeks since we took off on our twenty-seventh mission. It was during this period of time that my family was informed that we were missing in action. It had been seven weeks since all of our belongings had been moved out of our barracks and into the "death barracks" because no one knew if we would ever return. Just the mere fact that we were rescued did not guarantee our safe return

The Lady From Hell

to base. When we failed to return from our mission, a replacement crew took our bunks, in much the same way that our crew had done a long time ago. I remembered what it was like watching them take crewmembers' belongings and putting them into the "death barracks." What an eerie feeling it was. Collecting my own personal belongings from this very barracks brought these eerie feelings right back.

This time, we were assigned to an empty barracks, just the six of us. We did not mind, since we all got along very well. The war had brought us closer together, and we were indeed brothers. We exchanged war stories with our buddies long into the night. They were quite in awe of what we had gone through. They informed us that during the time we were gone, Chelveston had also gone through some changes. The crews now operated with only one waist gunner, as opposed to two. With constant protection from the P-51s, this did not matter much. The number of required missions, before a crew could go home, was increased to thirty-five; five more than when we had left. However, the missions were now short sorties, bombing in support of the army ground troops. Most of the time there was little or no flak, and only a few planes participated in these missions at a time. The Luftwaffe had completely vanished off the face of the earth. It seemed very different from the old days. Our buddies also told us the story about the Nazi flag that was hanging in our hangar. It was sent from an infantry division in a box, which contained a note. The note read as follows:

> "On this day, the 42nd Rainbow Division has entered and captured the German city of Schweinfurt. The flag enclosed is the same flag that flew over City Hall in the city of Schweinfurt. The Rainbow Division is proud to have avenged your losses."

Proportionately speaking, the United States Army Air Force lost more men than any other outfit during World War II. This is something of which I am not proud, but it is a fact. I have repeated the story of the Nazi

The Lady From Hell

flag because it meant so much to those of us who survived. Nothing could ever bring back the lives that were lost in the many missions over Germany. But maybe, just maybe, those who lost their lives did not lose them in vain.

It was quite late when we finally said goodnight to our friends. It had been a long day for us, and we had a meeting in the morning with the commanding officer. I was sure he would have a lot of questions for us. As I lay on my bunk, I kept thinking of the Schweinfurt raids, and how the 305th Bomb Group and the Eighth Air Force in particular, had suffered the worst losses of the war. I was sure that it was because of these heavy losses that the "big wigs" in Washington had changed their thinking regarding the heavy bombers. If the bombers were to hit and destroy their targets, they would need fighter escorts. Although the P-51s and P-47s finally arrived, it was too late for many crews. They never had the chance to retrieve their belongings, as I had done today.

I thought about my missions and about my long journey back. These were seven of the longest weeks of my life, but part of me appreciated the opportunity to see the wonderful cities in Europe. The war had destroyed a lot, but the beauty of the land and the hospitality of the people came through. However, this was all behind me now. As I lay in my bunk, I couldn't help but think how different things were back here at the base. Everything was so relaxed. It was almost as if we had come back to a different army, or even a different war. Or, perhaps, I was the one who was different.

22

GERMANY SURRENDERS

That morning, after breakfast, we had our meeting with our commanding officer. I noticed the calendar on his desk read May 7, 1945. We had been away for more than seven weeks. While we were gone, and during our entire ordeal, I never paid much attention to times or dates. This meeting lasted a little over an hour, and it was pretty much what we expected. One point we did get across was, that if we had a choice, we would prefer not to fly anymore combat missions. Usually crews that had been shot down did not have to return to combat. He smiled and replied that the missions of today were no longer what they used to be; however, he certainly understood our concern and would honor our wish. Regarding our future duties, he would get back to us. He could not make a commitment at that time, but he indicated that something very big would be happening very soon.

Right after the meeting, our crew went into the death barracks to recover the rest of our belongings. It was quite an eerie feeling; almost like you're attending your own funeral. I wondered why they kept it so dark and creepy looking there. They even hung dark blankets over the windows. I guess they did that to prevent someone from looking in. They called it a death barracks because once a plane was shot down very few crewmembers came back to claim their belongings. Some of my belongings were missing. Maybe they were lost, or maybe they were stolen. The person in charge informed me that a form could be filed for whatever items were missing, and they would be replaced. Most of my missing items were returned to me within a week. The only item they were unable to return was my beautiful brown leather jacket. It had bombs painted on the back, with the names of all the cities that

The Lady From Hell

I had bombed. I was advised that I would get a replacement as soon as a shipment of leather jackets came in. When this happened, I would have the bombs painted on the new jacket.

    I never got that new jacket because the very next day, on May 8, 1945, Germany surrendered. With that news, the 305th Bomb Group shut down and ceased combat operations. The B-17 Flying Fortresses had flown their last combat missions in Europe. No longer would we hear the drone of over one thousand Flying Fortresses and B-24 Liberators assembling. The skies over England would now be relatively quiet in comparison to how they were during the war. The 305th Bomb Group was one of the best groups in the Eighth Air Force, and I was certainly proud to be a part of it. But the price we paid was way too high as the news of Germany's surrender had come too late for a lot of my friends. I wished they were alive so that we could have shared this blessing together. The war that we had fought for so long had finally ended.

Frank J. Condreras

There were a lot of red eyes on that day at Chelveston. There were many of us who had lost friends in the war, and although the news was a blessing, many of us were saddened as we said prayers for those of us who did not make it. Ironically, with all that going on, I kept thinking about that infantry division that replaced us in Drew field, and the train ride we took together. Eventually, we wound up in Gulfport, Mississippi and they went to California, and the Pacific operation. I wondered how many of them had survived. I said a prayer for them also.

On that day, Chelveston was in complete chaos. No one knew what was going on, not even our leaders. Rumors circulated by the thousands: we were told that the next day there would be a meeting in the hangar, and everyone on the base was invited to attend. Our leaders would try to shed some light on the situation. The next day, practically the entire base showed up. There were flight crews, ground crews, mess hall personnel, doctors, nurses and

The Lady From Hell

orderlies from the hospital, people from the Military Police, file clerks, and office personnel from all the different outfits. Everyone was there. I don't know who was minding the store! The entire hangar was filled to capacity, and we all sat on the floor and listened to the words of wisdom. The news was not earth shattering. We were told that the base would continue to operate in the normal fashion, with one exception; there would no longer be any combat missions. Instead, skeleton crews would fly sightseeing tours to Germany for anyone on the base who wanted to see the destruction the big bombers had caused. Six to eight people would be assigned to each Flying Fortress. We would continue tours until ground personnel were accommodated. A skeleton crew consisted of the two pilots, the navigator, the flight engineer, and a radio operator. During the war, when a plane lost an engine in combat and a new one had to be installed, the plane had to fly a certain number of hours with the new engine before it went into combat. Since "The Lady

From Hell" had quite a few engine changes during combat, our skeleton crew did a lot of flying, including takeoffs and landings, to see how well the new engines handled at full power. We flew anywhere from four to six hours at a time, because it was the only way to be sure the engine was combat ready. It was during one of these flights, and under the watchful eye of my pilot, that I was afforded the opportunity to land "The Lady From Hell." This way, if both pilots were wounded or killed during a mission, I would be able to land the plane. I had seen hundreds of landings, and I knew what to do by heart. I could do it in combat if I had to. This point may have been academic anyway since we were so closely situated in the cockpit. If the pilots got hit, chances were I would also get hit. Fortunately, it never became an issue.

After Germany's surrender, for the sightseeing missions, we were assigned one of the spare Flying Fortresses, which we immediately named "The Lady From Hell #2." We had taken out the waste guns

The Lady From Hell

and covered the openings with Plexiglass to keep the plane warmer. The B-17 was not built to be a passenger airplane, but to make our ground personnel more comfortable we put boxes in the waist and the radio room, so they could sit when they got tired of standing.

To honor our ground troops, the 305th bomb group went all-out. We simulated the tours as if they were missions. From the briefing to flying formation with other Fortresses, we made them as real as possible. The only things missing were the bombs and the ammunition, and we were grateful for that. The first group we took on it consisted of six mechanics including our own ground crew. To say that they enjoyed it would be putting it mildly. They had a ball. I got a kick out of our crew chief, when we had him sit in the co-pilot's seat, and for several minutes he flew the plane, under the careful instruction of the pilot. There was a smile on his face from ear to ear, and when I saw him the next day he was still smiling.

Our second tour consisted of eight nurses from the base hospital. None of them had ever flown, and although they were a little bit afraid, they were delighted to be on board. Our flight plan called for about five hours of flying. Once over Germany, the pilot flew at very low altitudes so they could get a good look at the destruction the big bombers had caused. Some German cities were actually leveled. It was indeed sobering to see. While in-flight, we gave them a tour of the Flying Fortress. We showed them the tail gunner's position and the nose of the plane, and I showed them the top turret and how it operated. The pilot allowed those who wanted to sit in the co-pilot's seat, and he would let them fly the plane for several minutes. They all became pilots, and they were thrilled with everything they saw and did. They would certainly have something to write home about that night.

We performed these duties for several months. There were times when we would fly some high-ranking officers to different

The Lady From Hell

cities in Germany. Usually, these flights required staying overnight, and would sometimes take several days. We would also fly American soldiers, who had been prisoners of war, to a port of embarkment, so they could be sent home. One day, after returning from one of these tours, we were called into headquarters where we were told that we would have some choices to make. The 305th Bomb Group had been assigned a project that required photographing Europe, from different altitudes, to draw new maps. This would require former gunners to go to school and be trained as photographers. The project would last about a year, after which you may or may not receive a promotion. There would be lots of time off, and in a year the war in the Pacific should be over. It sounded like a good deal, and most of the crew agreed to stay for the assignment. I chose to go home. I had been away too long, and I had put my family through too much. I needed to see them and they needed to see me. I was told I would be sent to Fort Dix, get my one-month's leave, and then be assigned to B-29 flight engineer training. Upon completion of training, and because of my war record, I would graduate as an officer. I would then be sent to the Pacific theater of operations if the war was still going on. I had reasoned to myself that, by the time all of my training had taken place, the war in Japan should be over. In fact, even now, the war in the Pacific was winding down. Only time would tell if I had made a wise choice.

A week or so later, it finally happened. I was being sent to Southampton, England, where I would be boarding the Queen Elizabeth for my voyage back to the United States. I was being sent home!

The hardest thing I ever had to do was say goodbye to my crew. We had been together for such a long time, and we had done so many things together, that we were like family. During the war there were many times when we put our lives in each other's hands. We shook hands and hugged each other, and restated our promise that we

The Lady From Hell

would meet again somewhere in the United States, once we all got home. This never happened, unfortunately. Illness, family problems, financial difficulties, and job related issues, were some of the reasons we never again assembled as a group. Today, only four of the original ten are still living. Regardless, I think of all of them very often. In the entire Eighth Air Force, there was no better crew.

23

HEADING BACK TO THE U.S.A.

When I arrived at Southampton, I was told to report to a certain Pier where the Queen Elizabeth was docked. I was to board her as soon as possible. I had visions of a beautiful stateroom all to myself, or maybe sharing it with one other soldier, and enjoying a leisurely ride home. I also envisioned eating the best foods, and then relaxing on deck while waiting for my next meal. After all, I was going home on the largest luxury liner in the world. My bubble immediately burst when I arrived at the pier. There were masses of military personnel boarding the ship. I was told later that there would be almost five thousand troops on this voyage. Since I was one of the last to board, I was assigned to a room that was already occupied by five soldiers. In the room there were three bunks and three hammocks. I took the last hammock.

The room was designed to occupy two people, had it been used for a cruise. Since this was not a cruise, they packed us in like sardines. I was not complaining, however, since I was going home, and that was the bottom line. Besides, our room even had a porthole for ventilation, and at least we were above water level. There were others who were not as fortunate.

Although going home was what I had prayed for, and was now happening, the first few days of my trip were a downer. It had been only two days since I said goodbye to my crew, and already I was missing them. In addition, compared to flying, the Queen Elizabeth moved ever so slowly. In fact, everything on the big ship moved slowly. No matter what you did, you did it from the back of a long line. For breakfast, lunch, and dinner, you could wait anywhere from an hour to an hour and a half before you even got to where the food was being served. The Queen Elizabeth did not have the capacity to cook for the thousands of troops, so most of the meals

The Lady From Hell

consisted of sandwiches, potato salad, and coleslaw. There was plenty of fruit on board, including the canned variety. Coffee, tea, fruit drinks, and sodas comprised our drinks. My five new buddies, with whom I shared the room, were all from the infantry. They had all participated in the Battle of the Bulge. They didn't seem to mind waiting in line for their food because it was better than eating "K rations" out of a can. They did not care that the room was small, stuffy, and crowded, because it was better than sleeping on the hard ground, or in foxholes, in freezing rain and snow. It made me realize how lucky I was to be in the Air Force. No matter how tough a mission was, if we got back to base, we always had a hot meal waiting for us as well as a warm bed with clean sheets. That day, I counted my blessings.

Frank J. Condreras

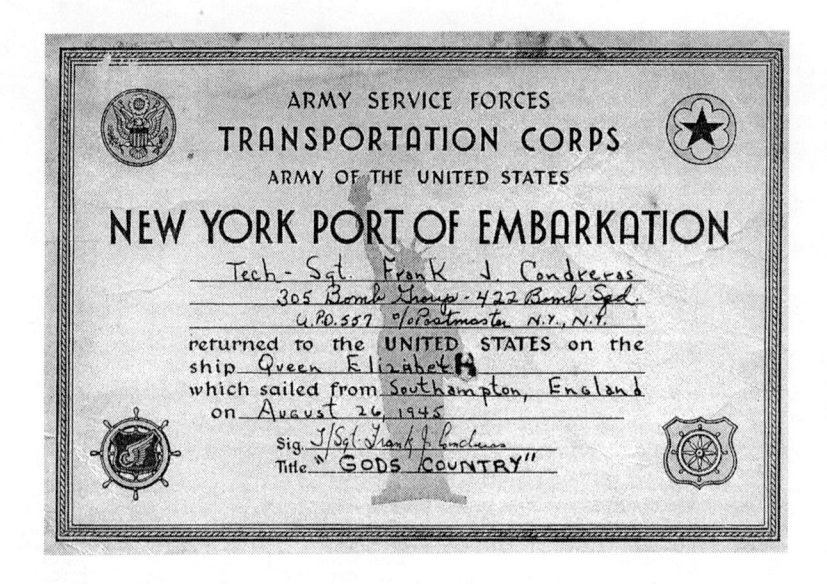

> **ARMY SERVICE FORCES**
> **TRANSPORTATION CORPS**
> ARMY OF THE UNITED STATES
>
> ## NEW YORK PORT OF EMBARKATION
>
> Tech-Sgt. Frank J. Condreras
> 305 Bomb Group - 422 Bomb Sqd.
> A.P.O. 557 c/o Postmaster N.Y., N.Y.
> returned to the UNITED STATES on the
> ship Queen Elizabeth
> which sailed from Southampton, England
> on August 26, 1945
> Sig. T/Sgt Frank J. Condreras
> Title "GODS COUNTRY"

Aboard the Queen Elizabeth, I did return safely to the good old U.S.A.

Good news came to us on our second day at sea. Japan had surrendered. I saw veteran soldiers crying, shaking hands, and hugging one another. It was a repeat performance of when Germany had surrendered; only the cast was different. It was what each of us had prayed for: no more fighting and no more lives lost. At long last, the world was at peace. There was no wild celebration on the Queen Elizabeth

The Lady From Hell

that day, but the looks on everyone's faces spoke volumes. Those of us who had bottles shared our drinks with those who did not. We all toasted that there would never be another war, for we had fought the war that was supposed to end all wars!

It was two days after we had received the news of Japan's surrender that we spotted land. We could see the United States. As we got closer, I could see Coney Island, Fort Hamilton, and Shore Road. These were all places that I could walk to from my home. On Shore Road there were thousands and thousands of people waving to the Queen Elizabeth. The papers had printed the names of all the military personnel who would be returning home on the Queen Elizabeth. Since we were among the first military personnel to return we got a rousing welcome. We could hear people shouting "Welcome home Yanks!" My family was among the thousands that were lining up along the streets of Shore Road. I could not see them, but my gut feeling told me they were there. As we steamed up the Narrows, into New York, we saw more and more ships of all kinds. There were fireboats that were spraying water in all directions and making beautiful designs. There were excursion boats that had a band playing military songs on the open decks. There were boats that were releasing thousands and thousands of red, white, and blue balloons, and the sky was full of them. Most of the boats carried huge signs welcoming us home. We were all very surprised and, in fact, some of us were in total shock. We were under the impression that no one knew we were coming home. As the party continued, more and more boats arrived. I must have counted eight to ten different bands playing alongside our ship. It was a site I will never forget. As we continued, very slowly towards New York, we spotted the Statue of Liberty. Since I was born in Brooklyn, I had seen her many times, but never before did she look more beautiful than she did on that day. She seemed to be saying "Welcome back." Most other soldiers on board were from all over

The Lady From Hell

the United States, and many of them had never seen the Statue of Liberty. They were in awe. They were looking at something that they would never forget. A nostalgic ending to a harrowing war experience, it was quite a sight.

The Statue of Liberty was a sight welcomed by many weary soldiers sailing into New York Harbor.

As we arrived at the pier at which we were to dock, the tugboats moved into position. It took several hours and a lot of patience to move this giant ocean liner into her slip. As we disembarked, there were thousands of people along the piers welcoming us home. Although not as many as were lined up along Shore Road, this group was a lot closer to us and a lot louder. There were bands, including several from high schools. It was clear that our homecoming was quite an event. It was a good feeling and we were all quite proud. I did not see my family when I got off the ship. Seeing them at the pier would have made the moment sweeter, but nothing could put a damper on the joy and relief I felt when I first stepped back on American land. All those moments of fear and doubt were gone. The war was over, and I was home.

It was quite obvious that Japan's surrender had caught everyone by surprise. There was mass confusion. Finally, after a long wait, I was advised that I was being sent to Greensboro, North Carolina, where my papers would be processed, and I would be discharged from the army. I didn't know why I was being discharged from Greensboro, except that maybe I had been registered to go to B-29 flight engineer training there. Personally, I could have

The Lady From Hell

cared less where I went. I was home and time was no longer my enemy. If it took a week longer or a month longer to get my discharge papers, I could have cared less. When I got to Grand Central station, I called my family and told them what was going on. I was back in the United States, and I was on my way to North Carolina to be discharged. I told them that it could take several weeks, but I would keep in touch and let them know exactly what was going on. Speaking to them, after all that time, gave me an incredible feeling of elation. The joy in their voices was evident, and I was immediately grateful that the ordeal I had put them through was over.

When I arrived at Greensboro, the confusion and inefficiency continued. The officer in charge said I should have reported to Fort Dix, picked up my discharge papers, and then come to Greensboro. I asked the dumb question, "If my papers were at Fort Dix, why was I not sent directly there to get discharged?" After three years in the Army no answer he could have given me would have surprised me. He told me that all Army Air Force personnel residing in the eastern section of the United States had to be discharged from Greensboro. I dared not ask why. He told me not to worry. They could get the papers sent from Fort Dix, and I would soon be on my way. I was assigned a bunk in a barracks that had only a handful of soldiers. These people were based at Greensboro, and had specific jobs to perform, so they would leave early in the morning and not come back until late afternoon. Most of the time, I was alone in this huge empty barracks. I did not mind, though. I got up when I pleased, and showered and shaved when I pleased. If I was awake and ready in time to eat at the mess hall, I would eat there. If I was late, I ate at the base's post exchange. It made little or no difference to me. I was no longer fighting the system. I was totally relaxed and enjoying the camp facilities. I kept in touch with my family, via letters and phone calls, twice a week. Even though they wanted me home, they took the delay

The Lady From Hell

in stride. About a month or so later, I was called into base headquarters. The officer was embarrassed to report that Fort Dix had sent my papers, but not all of them. He advised me that he could discharge me and send me to Fort Dix to pick up the rest of my papers. I would be free to go home from there. Again, I could have cared less. In fact, it was a rather fitting ending. The place where my military life began would be the same place it was going to end. The wheel had completed its full revolution, and I was ready to go on with my life. When I had reported to Fort Dix almost three years earlier, I said that someday I would return. Maybe God was granting my last wish in the Army.

24

THE DISCHARGE

I arrived at Fort Dix via a bus ride to Trenton, New Jersey, and a cab ride from Trenton to Fort Dix. Since the Army was paying, I was assuming the role of a big spender. At Fort Dix, I found the staff to be very efficient. My papers were quickly put in order, and the administrative problems I had were quickly resolved. My discharge was complete, and I could leave at any time I wanted. I was even issued a train ticket from Trenton to Grand Central station in New York. I asked the officer in charge if it would be possible to stay at Fort Dix an extra day. I recounted to him the story of how my Army life had started at Fort Dix, and it would have meant a lot to me to walk around the camp and relive some old memories from a long time ago. He indicated that this would really be against army regulations, but, with all the ribbons I had on my uniform, and the sacrifice I had made for my country, how could he refuse? He further advised me that if I wanted to remain overnight, there were clean bunks in barracks number 29. It was a nice gesture on his part, and I was very appreciative. I put my suitcases in barracks 29, near one of the empty bunks, and started out on my tour of Fort Dix. It would be the last day that I would ever spend in a United States Army Camp. Throughout the war, I had been in too many camps, and had spent more time in any of them than I spent here. But Fort Dix was different. It had started here, and it would be ending here.

    It had been a long time since my first visit, and it seemed as if a lot of changes had taken place. The camp itself was different. Everything seemed to be done at a much slower pace than it was years ago. I remember when I first arrived at the camp it was still in the process of being built. Trees were being cut down, new barracks were being built, and new sidewalks and streets were being paved. Everything was

The Lady From Hell

happening very quickly. Hundreds upon hundreds of new soldiers arrived daily, and within a week, these same soldiers would leave. There was a constant flow of men in and out. It was indeed a beehive of activity. Of course, the war was going on at that time, which probably had something to do with the busy pace.

    The first building I spotted was the officers' mess hall, where, after only three days in the army, I had been assigned KP I believed, at that time, that these initials stood for kitchen patrol, but whether this was correct or not, I never found out. The mess hall was closed as it had a big padlock on the front door. According to some soldiers who were based at Fort Dix, the mess hall had closed over a year ago. Standing here on this day prompted me to think back to what had transpired on my third day in the Army. It was Easter Sunday, and I was already missing my family. I had never been away from home much less missed a holiday. I had wondered what they would be doing. What would they be eating? Would they have company? In all the years that followed, I don't believe I was more depressed than I was on that Easter Sunday. I think the mess sergeant sensed this that day, or maybe he felt sorry for me, because after we finished our 16 hours of KP, he allowed me to use his office phone to call home. The only stipulation he made was that I keep the call under two minutes. I remember feeling so much better after the phone call. Although my mother and sister had cried, it was nice to hear their voices. My first bad day in the army was now behind me, and I had survived. Little did I know, at that time, that there would be many more bad days in the three long years that lay ahead. But, as time would tell, I would survive them as well. During my time at Fort Dix, I could have never imagined what lay in store for me.

    I spotted the movie house. It was no longer used to show movies about sexually transmitted diseases. It was now used for family entertainment. The medical barracks, where we received our shots and

The Lady From Hell

our physicals, were boarded up. They were now located in another building. Even the mess hall, where I had eaten my first meal, was boarded up with a big lock on the door. I will never forget that frozen bologna sandwich which constituted my first meal in the army. As I continued my tour, Fort Dix was appearing more and more like a ghost town. Many buildings had been closed and padlocked.

    I found my old barracks almost immediately. It was locked, but the officer that was on duty had given me the key. Being in there again gave me a funny feeling. The building had not been used for a long time. Everything was very dusty, and there was a musty smell in the air. I spotted my bunk right away. I knew it was my bunk because it was right under the first window. This was where it had all started. How scared I was then, that first night. How cold and hungry I was, and I kept thinking, what next? The quartermaster group had given us one blanket and a pillow, but no sheets or pillowcases. I'm sure we were being punished for our late arrival to camp. I remember the entire camp being angry with us for something over which we had no control. We received full bedding in the morning, but I was unable to sleep that night. I reminisced about all the things that had transpired that day. I remembered that intense feeling of sadness that morning at Grand Central station. That night, as I lay on my bunk, I could still hear people crying. By the time I fell asleep that night, it was four o'clock in the morning. One hour later, we were awakened by a sergeant bellowing so many orders it was hard to remember them all. It was quite apparent that my second day would be extremely busy.

I locked the door to the barracks and took the key back to the captain at headquarters. I thanked him for the privilege he had given me in allowing me to relive my past memories. He got up from his desk and said, "No, Sergeant. It is me who should be saying thank you for what you have done for us," and with that, he shook my hand. It was a good feeling. He also advised me that I was welcome to use the mess hall if I was hungry. I told him, "Captain, as long as they are not serving frozen bologna sandwiches, I would be happy to have lunch." We then shared a good laugh.

That same day I left Fort Dix. As I got to the front gate, I put my two suitcases down, and I turned around to get my last look at an army camp. I had been to many camps, but Fort Dix represented the beginning and the end of my military career. And, as had Fort Dix, I had changed a lot since the beginning. As I left Fort Dix, I realized that the Army had done its job. I was no longer afraid, nor was I cold or hungry. I had survived combat in a horrible war. I prayed for all my buddies who did not survive, and I prayed for their families. There were so many of them and, to this day, I think of them very often. Throughout the war, we kept hoping that this would be the war that would end all wars. At that time, this wish seemed reasonable.

Frank J. Condreras

Unfortunately, it turned out not to be the case.

> **Army of the United States**
>
> **Honorable Discharge**
>
> This is to certify that
>
> FRANK J CONDRERAS 32889656 Technical Sergeant
>
> 422nd Bombing Squadron (H)
>
> Army of the United States
>
> is hereby Honorably Discharged from the military service of the United States of America.
>
> This certificate is awarded as a testimonial of Honest and Faithful Service to this country.
>
> Given at AAF 3RD GREENSBORO NORTH CAROLINA
>
> Date 27 October 1945
>
> ODEA EVANS
> Lt Col A C

This certificate speaks for itself.

The losses we sustained in World War II were tremendous, depending on which reports you read. Almost seven hundred thousand never made it back and just as

The Lady From Hell

many were wounded, only to return home with arms, legs, and parts of their minds missing. Some eighty thousand were taken as prisoners of war, and are considered missing in action today. The totals are staggering, and this does not include the many families who continue to grieve. Still, wars continue, more soldiers die, and more families grieve. I don't think I will see world peace in my era, but I hope and pray you will see it in yours.

25

A CIVILIAN AGAIN!

As I was leaving Fort Dix and boarding the train in Trenton, New Jersey, I realized that I was no longer a crewmember. I was no longer a flight engineer, nor was I a Technical Sergeant. In fact, I was no longer a soldier. I was a civilian. This would be the last train ride for me for which Uncle Sam would be paying.

Train rides had become part of my Army life. I had arrived and eventually departed the many camps I had attended by train. Some rides were joyful and happy, while others were sad and depressing. I accepted both because I had no other choice. You took the good with the bad. Many times these trains would make unscheduled stops along the way, either by design or because of problems. More times than not the Red Cross would somehow know about the stops, and they would always be there with coffee and donuts for us. In the time that I had spent in the service, the Red Cross had become, and continues to be, my favorite charity.

The train ride home was beautiful, pulling into and out of every station quickly and quietly. It was a little different than that first day when I headed the other way to Fort Dix. Maybe I was enjoying the ride because I was riding as a civilian, not as a soldier. Even the conductor, who punched my ticket, leaned over and said, "Welcome home, Sergeant." I was feeling so comfortable that I dozed off into a sound sleep. The same conductor woke me up to advise me we were pulling into Grand Central station. The scene there was also a lot different than it was during wartime when it was somber and pensive. Now, people were laughing and telling jokes. Some were running to catch trains to go home, or perhaps to go to work. In the war years, there were no jokes, only tears and sorrow. What a difference a war makes. I could have taken the subway home, but I

The Lady From Hell

was still playing the part of the big spender, so I took a cab back to Brooklyn.

The cab driver was an elderly man. He asked me if I had been discharged and if I were coming home for good. "Yes," I replied, "I'm home for good. I'm finished with the Army." As I was talking to him, I noticed he had tears in his eyes. I thought maybe I had said something to disturb him, but I soon found out that he had a son in the United States Navy, about the same age as me. Unfortunately, his son would not be coming home. He had been killed in the battle of the Coral Sea. It was his only son and the hardest thing for him was going home at night to his grieving wife, and spending the night crying together for hours on end. I wish there was something I could have said or done to have made this man feel better. They say we won the war, but these people won nothing. They lost the only thing they valued more than life itself, their only son. Their lives would never be the same. When we reached our destination, I tried to give him a tip, but he would not accept it. It was his way of saying, "Welcome home." When I closed the door of the cab to say goodbye, I saw the tears running down his face. The war had caused many grown men to cry. It had become quite a common sight. I, too, had become misty-eyed for this cab driver, whom I did not even know. I did not want my family to see me looking depressed. I tried to compose myself, put on my happy face, and started up the stairs to my family.

It was early evening, and there was no one on the porch. I suspected they were having dinner. Several neighbors, who were outside their homes, spotted me and ran over to shake my hand and welcome me home. We hugged and kissed, and I was sure all that commotion would have alerted my family that I was home, but they apparently did not hear anything. It was better that way. My reception would be more private. I wanted to be alone with them the first time we met. I walked up the steps, rang the bell, and waited. It was my brother who answered the door,

The Lady From Hell

and when he saw me he screamed, "Mom, Frankie is home!" I don't remember much of what happened after that. I remember hugging my mother. She was crying, and I remember saying to her, "Mom, this is not a furlough. I'm not going back anymore. I'm home for good." As I held her, I could feel her body trembling.

My grandmother and my grandfather looked the same, except that they had gotten older looking. My brother, who was fifteen years old when I left for the Army, was now eighteen years of age. At least if they drafted him now, there would be no active combat for him. My father was the last to greet me, and did so with a big welcome-home grin. He kept staring at my ribbons, and I could tell he was very proud. He had a few medals of his own as a World War I veteran, and I was very proud of him. The family member that surprised me the most was my little sister. She had grown up into a little lady, and from what I could see, had taken over many of the household duties.

She was twelve years old, and I could not get over how mature she had become.

My dog Blackie had gotten older as well. He was no longer a puppy, and he was also a little heavier now. I thought to myself, "Blackie, we are going to do a lot of running in the park, and we will get those extra pounds off of you." He had such a happy look on his face when he saw me. His eyes seemed to say, "Stay with us. You have been away too long." Later in the evening, Blackie and I went out for a long walk. During the walk, he stopped several times to jump on me, with his paws almost on my shoulders. I guess he was making sure I was still there. When we returned from our walk, I sat on the steps of the porch. Blackie laid down next to me, with his head and his paws on my lap. In the years to come, I would spend a lot of quality time with Blackie. We had a lot of catching up to do. We stayed that way for almost an hour, until mom came to get us. She had cake and coffee ready, which I shared with Blackie. My family and I talked long

The Lady From Hell

into the night. There was so much to talk about. Finally, we all decided to go to bed. It was quite a long day, and it was very late. It did not take me very long to fall asleep. The last thing that I remember was Blackie lying on the side of my bed. When I woke up the next morning, he was still there. I think he was making sure that I was not leaving again.

As I woke up, I could smell the aroma of bacon and eggs coming from the kitchen. Although the Army food was generally good, the eggs were powdered, and the only way you could make powdered eggs was to scramble them. It would have been impossible to cook fresh eggs for thousands of soldiers, so we had to settle for powdered eggs. It was indeed a treat when mom made those fresh eggs, sunnyside up, with bacon and French toast on the side. It was a feast that I enjoyed tremendously. I ate six eggs that morning. Of course, my partner, Blackie, helped me with my breakfast. Right after breakfast, Blackie and I would be heading for the park where we would work off some of those eggs. When we returned from the park, both Blackie and I were huffing and puffing.

Now that I was home, the first thing I wanted to do was to buy some civilian clothes. When I was discharged, I had 'mustering out pay' that I was given. The clothes I had from almost three years ago no longer fit, and besides, they were out of style. So, I went shopping. I bought two suits, each of which had two pairs of pants, and I also bought a couple pairs of slacks. I bought a pair of shoes and a pair of sneakers. A couple of shirts and ties completed my shopping spree. I still had about two hundred dollars left, and I was now set for civilian life.

Since I had been among the first servicemen to be discharged, I had time to rediscover Brooklyn before most of the other soldiers came home. Two or three years before the war, I had noticed that Brooklyn was changing. The horse-drawn wagons were practically gone. My dad, who worked for a milk company, still had his horse

The Lady From Hell

and wagon, but there was talk that they, too, would be replaced very shortly with trucks. The era of the horse-drawn cart, as the primary means of transportation, was rapidly coming to an end.

One day, as I was coming home from a walk with Blackie, one of the neighbors spotted me and insisted that we go to the tavern to have a drink. Although I wasn't a drinker, I went along with him. There were quite a few people at the bar who had heard that I had been discharged, and they were all offering to buy me a drink, even the owner of the bar. I stayed about an hour, thanking them all, and headed home. If I had stayed much longer, I would have gotten loaded. Still, it was a nice feeling to know that so many people cared. I was hoping the feeling would be the same for all the servicemen as they returned home from the far corners of the world.

26

THE CHANGING TIMES

In the three years that I had been away, Brooklyn had become a city within a city. Even before I left for the service, I had noticed that many families were moving into Brooklyn, and many of the wide-open spaces were disappearing. A lot of the empty lots were now becoming homes.

Trucks were replacing the horse-drawn wagons in record numbers. The milk companies were the last to hold out, but in the end, they too replaced their horses with trucks. So my dad was driving a truck instead of the horse-drawn wagon. He missed his horse, I could tell, because he would tell stories of how his horse followed him from block to block without so much as a command, while he made his deliveries. The horse would always stop at the corner of any block, and wait for my father to give him the command to cross the street. As a child, I was lucky enough to go for rides on his wagon. I will always cherish those rides my dad gave me on those special days.

During the war many factories had opened in Brooklyn. They were called either war plants or defense plants, depending on what items they produced. These plants offered numerous job opportunities, and many families moved to Brooklyn in search of these lucrative jobs. The Brooklyn Navy Yard also contributed to the population explosion.

The streets had cars parked on both sides, leaving no room for ball playing of any kind. Where do the kids of today play ball? How about the following generation, with even less room? I guess sacrifices will have to be made. Schoolyards and parks are still available, but it could never be the same, because my ballpark was right in front of my house. Of course, with the population explosion, came bigger and bigger business. More and more cars and trucks appeared to service these big businesses. Traffic lights were being installed to ensure the smooth

The Lady From Hell

flow of traffic and to avoid accidents with pedestrians crossing the street. As I was growing up, I don't recall anyone getting run over by a horse!

The mom-and-pop stores were disappearing as quickly as the horses. Huge stores, called self-service stores, began opening up. People who would shop at the stores would have to pick their own items from the well-stocked store shelves. People started to descend on the stores in masses, because shopping like this saved money. With the refrigerator replacing the old icebox, people were able to shop once a week instead of every day. This, in turn, put a lot of mom-and-pop stores out of business. There was no longer a grocer, a bakery, a meat market, or a fruit and vegetables store on every block. It had become quite obvious that the "little guy" could not compete with big business. Some stores lasted a little longer than others, but gradually changes took their toll. Very few mom-and-pop stores remained in business.

On my corner, the trolley car no longer

ran. This was the same trolley that had taken my father to work for many years, and the same trolley that would wait for him if he was running a little late. The conductor would even ring his bell to remind my father to hurry. Ironically, we only lived a few houses away from the trolley car stop. During the winter months, when the weather was inclement, my dad would wait in the hallway of our house listening for the trolley car bell, and when he heard the bell, that was his cue to get moving. The tracks for the trolley have since been ripped up, the street repaved, and buses have replaced the old trolley cars.

    The changes continued. There had been talk for some time about a bridge being built across the Narrows, linking the boroughs of Brooklyn and Staten Island. The bridge was going to be called the Verrazano Narrows Bridge. Once completed, it would be the longest expansion bridge in the world. It would run from Fort Hamilton in Brooklyn across to Staten Island. It wasn't long ago that the Queen Elizabeth

The Lady From Hell

had passed Fort Hamilton, with me and my fellow returning veterans, en route to New York City. If the bridge had been built then, the Queen Elizabeth would have passed right under it. In the process of building this bridge, many homes, on both sides of the bridge, would have to be destroyed to accommodate the exit and entrance ramps. Some families had lived in these homes for many years, some for their entire lives. Their homes had been passed on from generation to generation, but it made no difference to the "system." If you were standing in the way of progress, and the "system" wanted you out, you were out. They offered what they called a fair price for the homes in the area, and homeowners could either accept it or take them to court to try to get a better price. At the end of the process, only the lawyers made out. Usually, homeowners were forced to accept the first offer, and, in most cases, got the short end of the stick. Such was the price paid as Brooklyn expanded. Sooner or later, we would all be affected by it. Despite the sacrifices made by so many, today, the Verrazano Bridge is truly a wondrous site. It hosts thousands of cars and trucks; however, during most of the day, around all the exits and entrances there are huge traffic jams. Even progress has its drawbacks.

Before the bridge was constructed, the only link between the boroughs of Brooklyn and Staten Island was the ferry. The ferry usually ran every hour during daylight hours, including weekends. At night, departures ran every two or three hours. When you took the ferry in the daylight, the New York City skyline was a thing of beauty to behold. You could even get a good look at the Statue of Liberty from the ferry. But as good as the view was in the daylight, the view at night was breathtakingly spectacular. The lights that illuminated the city and its buildings were unbelievable. I know it is hard to believe, but the price of the ferry ride was five cents. I don't believe there was a better bargain in the entire world. When you took the ferry, it made no difference whether it was winter or summer. In the summer, you could stand on any of its decks, and in the winter, you could stay in the warm cabin and look out at the views from the big windows. On the water, you could also see the big ocean liners or steamers riding up and down the Narrows, either coming from or going to the piers in New York City. Today, there is still a ferry that operates from New York City to Staten Island, however the fare is no longer five cents.

The ferry also served as a setting for romantic interludes. You could take your girl on the ferry to Staten Island and buy hot chocolate in the cold weather or a cold soda in the summer. Then when you were back in Brooklyn, you would go to a movie and an ice cream parlor. Even when money was scarce, you could be with your girl about five hours, and it would cost about three dollars.

Coney Island was also a victim of growing pains. As a little boy, I remember crowds at the beach. Yet no matter how crowded, there was still a lot of room for people to open a blanket and relax. The sand was always clean and white looking, and you would have to walk almost the length of a city block to get to the water. When you got there, the water was so clear you could see schools of small fish swimming close to the shore. Small children would catch fish, put them in jars, and take them home as pets. Unfortunately, the fish usually died long before the children got home. When I went back to Coney Island's beaches after coming home from the war, there were wall-to-wall people, with no room for walking. The distance between the boardwalk and the water had greatly diminished, and the water was cloudy.

You could never mention Coney Island without mentioning Nathan's, the home of the best hotdog and fries in the world. This seemed to be the consensus throughout Brooklyn. Certainly, you could not beat the prices. The hot dogs were five cents each, and the French fries cost only ten cents. The roast beef sandwiches were also delicious, and they also cost ten cents. It

The Lady From Hell

was an affordable feast for everyone, young and old alike. There were times when I would use my last nickel, which I had been saving for the trolley car ride home, on that delicious hotdog. As good as the hotdog was, I would often regret that long walk home. At least I could take comfort in the fact that, while many things had changed while I was away, Nathan's remained the same.

On hot summer weekends, the newspapers claimed that as many as one million people would visit Coney Island. The beach was once described as a wall-to-wall carpet of people. Whatever you did, you did it on a long line. But despite the lines, there was no place like Coney Island in the world.

27

GETTING REACQUAINTED

Changes continued, not only in Brooklyn, but all over. In the army we had a saying, "Go with the flow." I had changed a lot since I had left Brooklyn three years ago, but I was determined to return to a normal life. My friends were now coming home from all corners of the world, and they too had been changed by their experiences. Every week or so, one or two of my friends came home, and after about six months, we were all back in Brooklyn; all, that is, who made it home. Some of my friends had made the ultimate sacrifice. They never returned home. Those lucky enough to make it back to Brooklyn came from all branches of the service. They had seen their share of the war, but we all tried to put it behind us as we looked forward to new and better times in our civilian lives.

One of my friends came home from

the war with a mental disorder. When we would go out in a group, we noticed he would often stare into space, almost as if in a trance. When we went bowling we would constantly have to remind him it was his turn to bowl. At times, he would wander to other parts of the bowling alley and someone would have to go after him. During the war, he was stationed with an advanced medical unit. It was a mobile army surgical hospital unit located near the frontlines. Every day, soldiers would arrive from the frontlines torn up and bleeding, some without arms or legs, and some beyond help. He witnessed these horrors on a daily basis. Gradually, it took its toll on him. And once he was home, his mental health continued to decline. He was eventually institutionalized. Asking his parents how he was doing was very difficult. They would visit him every weekend without fail, and they would come home very disappointed every time. I visited him several times, and there were many times when he did not recognize me. It was obvious that he was

The Lady From Hell

not getting any better. He remained in this institution for as long as I could remember. I often wondered if he ever realized the war was over, or if he was still fighting it in his mind.

Another friend of mine had contracted malaria while fighting the Japanese in the Burma China operations. He never looked well, and took medication for as long as I knew him. He would get jaundiced and have that look associated with the condition. He would live with these medical problems the rest of his life. A lot of people said we were lucky to be home and alive. This was probably true, but some of us were luckier than others. Regardless, we all lost three years of the best years of our lives. No one could give those years back to us. Experience had given us a deeper appreciation for our homes, our families, and our friends. It was good to be together again. It had been a long time, and things were certainly not the same now. Before we left for the war, we were kids, but the war had changed us all. It made some of us men, but it cut others down in the prime of their lives, or left them with physical or mental ailments that would plague them for the remainder of their days. In our conversations, my friends and I very seldom discussed the war. It was a subject we wanted to put behind us. It had already consumed enough of our lives.

My friends and I spent our time reminiscing about some of the crazy things we did as we were growing up. We used to build fires in the street. One of us would borrow some coal from our parent's coal bin, while someone else stole potatoes from the vegetable store. Our intention was to eat hot baked potatoes, but more often than not, we would be eating burned potatoes since we put them right into the fire. They still tasted good, though. There were times when five or six of us would compile our pennies to get 10 cents worth of the previous day's buns. The baker would give us a bagful, since he was happy to get rid of the stale buns. We would go down to someone's basement and have a party, and if someone had a cigarette, we would take

The Lady From Hell

turns puffing on it. In those days, smoking was the thing to do. Cigarettes cost a penny each at that time. With 10 cents we could buy a pack of "Wings" cigarettes, which were half-price. We were very efficient at pooling our resources and getting as much as we could for every penny. Hopefully, our skills would someday serve us well in the business world.

There were many times we did some stupid and dangerous things. Whenever we went to or from Coney Island, in order to save a nickel, we would hitch a ride by hanging onto the back of the trolley. Many times, the conductor would stop the trolley and chase us. If we had slipped or fallen while the trolley was in motion, we could have very easily been run over. Getting to Madison Square Garden, Ebbet's Field, Yankee Stadium, or the Polo Grounds, was a lot easier since it only required us to take the train. It was far easier to duck under the turn style or jump over it than to hitch a ride on the back of the trolley car. Most of the time the train conductor did not think it was worth his time or effort to chase us. Once at the different stadiums, we would pay the minimum admission and sit in seats where nosebleeds were possible. As the game progressed, we would look for empty seats below and work our way down, sometimes getting to field level.

Growing up, we did act recklessly at times, but we never hurt anyone intentionally. Hitching rides to save a nickel was dumb. Stealing was also wrong, regardless of how cheap potatoes were. We learned our lesson, and left these antics behind, along with our childhood. We grew up to be responsible adults.

Three years was a long time to be away from friends with whom you had grown up. The reunion was a fun time and we were enjoying each other's company. Before the war, we did a lot of things together, such as bowling, skating, going to the movies, and playing miniature golf. We would visit Coney Island and all the professional ballparks, including Madison Square Garden, and now, we were doing

The Lady From Hell

it as adults. We no longer ducked under the turn styles, or hitched rides on the back of trolleys. Every now and then one of us would commandeer the family car, and we would go in style. None of us had jobs yet. Some of my friends would soon be going back to school, while the others would be looking for jobs. We just wanted to spend a little time together, while it was still ours to enjoy.

We also started playing ball together again, but now we were playing softball instead of baseball. The balls were a little larger, and the running distances were a little shorter. Softball had become quite popular, replacing baseball as the number one sport among us "semi-professional" players. There were many reasons it had become so popular. One reason was that you could play it on cement in most schoolyards. This made many more fields available, allowing more teams to participate. Also, schoolyards were a lot closer to home than most city parks. In addition, you did not need all the equipment necessary in baseball. All you needed was a baseball cap, a tee shirt, and a pair of sneakers. A fielder's glove completed the uniform. The different taverns and restaurants in the neighborhood sponsored many of the teams, and they would buy the team uniforms advertising their businesses. I liked softball because playing on cement was so much cleaner than playing in parks covered with dust and dirt. Another plus was that the games were only seven innings long, and it took less time to play a game. The pitcher threw underhanded and with much velocity. The better the pitcher, the better the team. We were fortunate to have a very good pitcher, which made us one of the better teams around. After the games, we would go to the tavern that sponsored our team, and drink beer, discussing the game until it was time to go home to eat. Ball playing had become part of our lives again, and we were gratefully enjoying the game and each other's company, very much as we did before the war.

28

THE JOB SEARCH

Money started to become a problem with many veterans in the months after the war. New York State had what they called a 52-20 club. Simply stated, it meant a veteran could receive $20 a week for fifty-two weeks, or until he or she found employment. It was not a king's ransom, but it certainly helped. New York State had done for us what our federal government had failed to do.

The government had promised anyone who had a job prior to being drafted into the service that his or her job would be waiting for them upon their return. This was the way it should be. But for those of us who had just graduated high school, or for those who had been in college, there was no job to come home to. Right after the war the defense plants and war factories were closing down as fast as they had sprung open. Even the Brooklyn Navy Yard was laying off workers by the thousands. This swelled the unemployment market, so not only did we have to contend with incredible competition from the number of people looking for work, but also with those who had work experience. The returning young soldier already had two strikes against him.

The only experience I had was at being a flight engineer on the B-17 Flying Fortress. Thank God there was no more need for this type of work. The first thing I had done upon my return from the service was to apply to all the major airlines for a flight engineer position. They did not, however, recognize or honor the Army Air Force's certification for flight engineers. What the airlines required was an FAA-approved "A" and "E" certificate. The "A" certificate applied to the aircraft part of the plane, while the "E" certificate applied to the engine portions of the aircraft. To get the certificates, you had to attend an FAA approved program. The Army's program was not considered an approved program.

The Lady From Hell

After attending such a program and earning the certificates, the airline would hire you as a mechanic. After working for two years as a mechanic, you would then be allowed to apply for the first flight engineer school that became available. At this time, the airlines also required their mechanics to be "A" and "E" certified. Since there were thousands of unemployed people who had worked in the war factories making airplanes, who already had their "A" and "E" licenses, my chances were slim. The only way I could get my licenses was to attend one of the FAA approved schools. The closest one to me was the Academy of Aeronautics, located close to La Guardia airport in Queens, New York. The daytime program would take me two years, and if I chose to go at night, it would take five years.

I had filled out countless applications, went on numerous interviews, and still the ending was the same. It was as if I was listening to a recorded message. After completing my application, someone would interview me and, although the faces of the interviewers may have changed, their message was always the same. They were very proud of my fantastic war record; however, they were looking for someone with a little more experience. They would keep my application on file, and if anything came up, they would contact me immediately. It was a nice way of saying, "Thanks, but no thanks." In all fairness to the interviewer, my application showed very little experience. I was a high school graduate when I was drafted, and barely at that, and my Army experience carried very little weight in my search for employment in the civilian world.

When the war ended, the airlines, as well as other businesses, had a huge selection of applicants from which to choose, many with good credentials and skills. If the shoe were on the other foot, and I was doing the interviewing, I would also pick the most experienced, qualified applicant. It made good business sense. Still, I was hurt each and every time I was rejected. It was humiliating, and I

The Lady From Hell

had become discouraged and depressed. Maybe I had made a mistake. Maybe I should have stayed in the Air Force after the war had ended. I had a good ranking, and the pay was good. But, more importantly, I had the respect of both my peers and subordinates. That was a good feeling and it was something I did not have in civilian life.

In all fairness, our government did offer to pay for our education, and some of my friends did take advantage of this offer. I wanted to further my education as well, but I needed to spend a year or two helping my family financially. After that, I would certainly go back to school. I had a very close friend with whom I had graduated, and he was having the same problems as I was in the employment search. During the war, he was a paratrooper, and had jumped behind German lines several times including on "D" day. Despite the fact that our sacrifices and efforts had helped to ensure the continuation of our democratic society, it seemed to mean very little now that we were home. A young soldier, with no work experience, had little chance of finding a good job.

In the meantime, Brooklyn continued to grow, thanks mainly to the people who had worked in the war plants during the war. These were the people who were buying up the empty lots and building new homes, buying new cars, and going into businesses. I would be lying if I said I was not envious. I realized they worked very hard and, at times, long hours for everything they had earned. I also realized that, without them, we would have never won the war. The war provided ample opportunity to make money in the defense plants. I was hoping that Uncle Sam would now come through for the struggling soldier. A bonus would have been great, but if not, then I would have taken a loan that I could pay back at a later date. There were rumors that the government was going to give us bonuses. The amounts would vary according to our respective branch of service. Unfortunately, these bonuses never came, and the most

The Lady From Hell

we were offered were low interest loans for school. What we needed was a push to get started, and to help us compete. Our government never answered our needs. To Uncle Sam, we were just a number.

Finally, I received some good news. My friend's brother was going to open up a shoe factory in the terminal market in Brooklyn. Of course, this meant my friend would have a job, and I as his friend, would also have a job. I had waited for so long for something good to happen, and now it was finally happening. Ironically, my friend's brother had worked in the Brooklyn Navy Yard during the entire war. He had boasted to me several times how he would work twenty and thirty, and even forty hours of overtime, at double and triple his normal wage. He was making good money to begin with, and the money he earned during the war enabled him to open his shoe factory. It did not matter now, because I had a job, and that was more important to me than anything else. I would have a paycheck every week! My mother no longer had to sneak a $10 bill into my pocket so that I could take my girlfriend to a movie and a pizza parlor. In fact, I would be able to give her some money each week. Since I had no experience operating any of the machines at the shoe factory, my friend put me in charge of the shipping department. It was not much of a job, but I would be making several dollars above minimum wage. I stayed with this job for almost a year, when I started to realize that I was going nowhere, simply because there was nowhere to go. It was at this time that I started to think about going back to school. Since the government was going to pay for my education, why not take advantage? God knows my government had taken advantage of me! I would continue to work my daytime job, and I would attend school at night. It would be difficult, and there would be long and tiring days during the next five years. I would have loved to have gone to school as a full-time student, but I just could not afford it. I needed that weekly paycheck.

The Lady From Hell

This was the group that graduated from the Academy of Aeronautic, despite the fact that many more had started with us. I'm seated in the center.

That fall, I started a new life. I wanted so badly to prove to my family that I could make it in the business world, and I was intent on succeeding. The first year, I was all gung-ho! School days were sixteen hours long, and I went three times a week. The most tiring part of the entire day was the long commute to and from school from work. Coming home at night required taking two trains and a bus, and with the light schedules that ran at night, it would take more than two hours from Flushing to Brooklyn. School was good, and I was doing well. I was surprised at how much my flight engineer training applied to what I was learning at the academy. I was not a genius, but I was a solid 'B' student. I had met someone in the class, and we became very good friends. He was an older man who was working in the stock room for one of the larger airlines. He was going to the academy to get his "A" and "E" licenses. He wanted to be a mechanic so he could make more money. I was surprised when I heard the amount of money the mechanics were making. You could live a mighty comfortable life with that kind of money. We shared stories of our families, and sometimes we even helped each other with our homework. We had become very good friends.

One night, I had gotten to school early. I was sitting in the cafeteria having a sandwich and a soda when he barged in all excited. He advised me there was a notice on the bulletin board, at his job, advertising

The Lady From Hell

an opening. It was in the crew-scheduling department. One of the requirements was that the applicant had to be familiar with handling crewmember problems. Since I had been a crewmember, I might have a shot at the job. He encouraged me to try for it, reminding me I had nothing to lose. He was a nice guy, and a good friend.

I started out very early the next morning. I wanted to be the first applicant interviewed. I was about an hour early for the interview, so, after completing my application, I sat down and waited. I was praying that this interview would not end in the same manner that all my other interviews had. I waited a long time, when someone finally came out and advised me that the person who usually conducted the interviews had called in sick that day. Instead, I would be interviewed by the chief pilot. I didn't know if that was a good omen or a bad one, but, like my friend said, I had nothing to lose.

Once again God had smiled on me, as He had done so many times in my life. The chief pilot had been a B-17 pilot who flew with the Eighth Air Force in England. We had so many things in common. We were both with the 305th Bomb Group, we were both based at Chelveston, and we had both been shot down over Germany. I could not have asked for a better interview, as we formed an instant bond, and I was hired on the spot. He laughed and told me to go home and enjoy the weekend. I would start Monday morning. It was, without a doubt, one of the happiest days of my life. I was working for a major airline, and being a flight engineer would become a reality instead of a dream. Did I mention that my starting salary would be twice what I was making at the shoe factory?

This was the beginning of a new and wonderful life for me. It would be almost thirty-five years later, when I would accept early retirement from this very same company.

The Lady From Hell

Becoming a civilian again meant wearing a suit of a different kind. Here I was working in crew scheduling at JFK Airport.

MY NEW LIFE

After I had gotten the job with this large airline, my life started to change considerably. What a difference a good paying job makes! I no longer felt like a misfit, but rather like I belonged. My army life and its memories were fading into the past, and for the first time since the war, I felt like a civilian. I could go wherever I wanted since money was no longer an issue. Now, after my girl and I went to a movie, or a play in the city, or some sporting event, we would go to the finest restaurants. I had forgotten how good it felt to eat off of clean tablecloths and linen napkins, instead of paper ones. No more pizza parlors and no more worrying if I would have enough money to pay the bill and leave a tip.

One of the first things I had to do when I got the job was to buy more clothes. I bought three suits, each with two pairs of pants, making it look like I had six suits. This was important since I would wear a different suit every day in the office. It made good sense. As the weeks and months passed, I would add to my wardrobe. There was nothing holding me back anymore. If I was a civilian, I was going to be a well-dressed civilian! My job was progressing nicely. I got along well with my co-workers and with the crewmembers. The chief pilot who hired me continued to treat me well, occasionally taking me out to lunch and telling me I was doing a good job. My office was both spacious and clean, with windows all around. It made for a very pleasant atmosphere. It was a little bit different than the factory from where I had come. All the big machinery banging away, the sewing machines going full blast, and people yelling above the noise so they could be heard, made for a very high noise level. I was glad I was no longer a part of that operation.

My job was to basically make sure that all flights that left LaGuardia, Kennedy,

The Lady From Hell

and Newark airports had a qualified crew on each flight. Since there were arriving flights that had turnarounds, it was important to monitor their arrival times to make sure they could protect their turns without delay. Mechanical problems, traffic problems, and weather delays were three issues that needed to be addressed. It was my job to have ample crews available to minimize delays as much as possible. Another problem was equipment changes. Sometimes, because of mechanical problems, it would be necessary to change the aircraft. Since the company operated several different kinds of airplanes, crews had to be matched to equipment based on proper qualification. In addition to all this, we had to make sure we were within the limitations of the pilot's contract and company policy. All in all, we had some very busy but interesting days.

Things continued to progress smoothly for me. I had been in the office over one year, and I had received two pay raises. I also had received pass privileges, which meant I could travel at no cost, depending on space available. I could travel anywhere in the world that my airline serviced. Like in basic training, I had kept a low profile, and did everything asked of me. There were times, in fact, when I went above and beyond what was asked of me. I had done well, and I was well liked by the company, the crewmembers, and my co-workers.

Although it was becoming very difficult, I was still attending night classes at the Academy of Aeronautics. I missed many classes because there were times when I had to work the night shift, but I managed to keep up with these classes. Although my grades were no longer in the mid-80s or '90s, at least I was still passing. My office was open seven days a week, 24 hours a day. This was the reason that shift work had become part of my life. Still, I wanted those "A" and "E" licenses. I knew that once I had them, I had enough pull in the company to forego the requirement of having to be a mechanic for two years. I would be put into the first flight engineer

The Lady From Hell

school available. Even though it would be a very long three years, it would be worth every minute.

After working a little over two years, I had saved enough money to buy a car. My family owned a car that they would let me use whenever I went out with my girl, but this was going to be my car. I had never owned anything of value that I could call my own, but now I would have a car. I could not afford a new car, so I bought a used one. It was two years old, and a very good bargain. It had been previously owned by someone in my family. The car would be a blessing, as I would no longer have to take two trains and a bus to get to work and to school. The car would cut my travel time in half and give me more time to study and do homework. I was quite proud to be the owner of a car. I took good care of it, and it took very good care of me. I had mixed emotions when I eventually traded it in for a new car, which my girl and I were buying each other for our wedding present. Yes, that's right, a wedding present! I

Frank J. Condreras

had started dating someone when I was working at the shoe factory. Her name was Mary, and it was love at first sight for me. We continued to date, and we eventually got engaged and then married.

This is me with my beautiful bride-to-be, Mary, at our engagement party.

The next three years of my life were miraculous. So many good things happened to me that it was hard to keep track of them. I had completed over five years in the airline industry, I had become a supervisor

The Lady From Hell

of my department, and I no longer worked night shifts. I worked strictly day shifts, with all holidays and weekends off. I finally completed my course work at the Academy of Aeronautics, but because I missed a lot of time, it took me five very long years. I received both my "A" and "E" licenses upon passing the FAA tests. I went home and put them in a drawer, and that is where they stayed. After all that planning, all that hard work, and all those long nights, I never used the licenses. There were two reasons for this. First, the airline for which I worked was not going to have a flight engineer school for several years because they were overstaffed in the flight engineer department. By that time, I would be over thirty years of age, and therefore, over the age limit. In those days, there were no laws regarding age discrimination. Second, I was now head of my own department. It was a great consolation. I went to work every morning in a clean suit, and I came home every night in a clean suit. Coming home every night was now very important to me, because my beautiful girlfriend had become my beautiful wife. While part of me was sad about never becoming a flight engineer, my priorities had changed.

Mary and I were married on December 6, 1953.

We had bought a new car, and soon we would be buying our new home. The rest of my family came a little later with the birth of two beautiful daughters. We eventually bought our home and settled in a little town on Long Island. Everything for which I had hoped and prayed, throughout the entire war, was coming true. The Army

The Lady From Hell

and the war no longer dominated my life. My number one priority was my beautiful family. My future would be dedicated to taking care of them and ensuring their well-being.

In 2003, Mary and I celebrated our 50th wedding anniversary with our family and friends.

EPILOGUE

Although I am not very good at giving speeches, it was my daughter's persistence in asking that landed me in front of forty high school students talking about World War II and my involvement in it. My daughter, Linda, is a teacher at a local high school on Long Island, and the students to whom I spoke amazed me with their attentiveness and receptiveness. I guess that learning from a textbook and listening to stories first-hand are very different.

I get the impression that students think that the United States of America was always a world power. At the start of World War II, nothing could have been further from the truth. Depending on which newspaper report you read, our army totaled anywhere from two hundred thousand to two hundred and fifty thousand. It was not an army that was equipped for modern warfare. Smaller countries, such as Belgium, Poland, Czechoslovakia, Hungary, Romania, Italy, and Spain had bigger and better equipped armies than we did at the start of the war. There were certainly no comparisons with the giants of that era such as Great Britain, France, Germany, Russia, China and Japan. We did have a good navy, which was listed as number three in the world behind Great Britain and Japan. This, however, was before Pearl Harbor.

By the end of World War II, our armed forces had grown to almost thirteen million strong, which is quite a difference from where we started. We had indeed become number one in world power, and we have kept that distinction to this day.

Tom Brokaw wrote a book calling my generation one of the greatest that society had ever known. My generation survived the stock market crash on Wall Street and the horrible depression that followed. We survived the horrible recession that followed the depression. We fought two wars at the same time against two of the most feared countries the world had ever known. Against tremendous odds, we won those

The Lady From Hell

two wars, one in the Pacific, the other in Europe. Unfortunately, my generation paid a heavy price for these victories. Losing four or five years of the prime of your life is a sacrifice, but absolutely nothing compared to those who made the ultimate sacrifice of life itself.

On occasion, someone will ask me if I'm bitter about losing those prime years of my life to World War II. No, I am not bitter. I'm grateful that I came home, and in one piece at that. Yes, I would have loved to have gone to college when I graduated from high school. Unfortunately, my generation did not have that option. The government did promise us an education after the war, but like many of us, I had to work to help support my family financially.

So, as I said, I went to school at night, after working all day. It was not the same as going to college during the day while enjoying the campus life at only a mere eighteen years of age. I was twenty-three, and there were no sports teams, there were no parties or dances after classes, and there

Frank J. Condreras

was no normalcy as we know it today. I do miss what might have been...

About the Author...

Tech. Sgt. Frank J. Condreras
United States Army Eighth Air Force

Frank was drafted into the army shortly after his Brooklyn high school graduation. After basic training in Florida, he then attended airplane mechanic school in Amarillo, Texas, and gunnery school in Kingman, Arizona. Serving in the Eighth Army Air Corps, he was a flight engineer and top turret gunner on a B-17G Flying Fortress called "The Lady From Hell." Heavily involved in the air war over Germany, Frank

Frank J. Condreras

and his fellow crewmembers successfully completed twenty-six missions, participating in Ardennes, Rhineland, and Central Europe campaigns. During his twenty-seventh mission, a bomb run over Jena, Germany, Frank was shot down. It was March 17, 1945. The plane crashed in Poland, where Frank was picked up by Russian infantry and held as a "Prisoner of War" until his status could be identified as U.S. Military. The crew spent two long months making their way back to base in Chelveston, England.

During his tenure in the service, Frank received the following medals:

Wings over Blue Velvet Patch: Indicates combat flying.

Presidential Citation: Given to his group for participating in bombing bridges over the Rhine River, stopping German reinforcements.

Air Medal with Four Oak Leaf Clusters: For completing 27 combat missions.

The Lady From Hell

Good Conduct Medal: Almost everyone got one of these.

Three Campaign Medals:
1. Battle of the Ardennes (with Bronze Star)*
2. Battle of the Rhineland (with Bronze Star)*
3. Battle of Central Germany (with Bronze Star)*
    *Bronze Star indicates combat in these areas

Sharp Shooter Medal: Given for Pistol, Rifle, and Carbine

Prisoner of War: Given to all Prisoners of War

Frank was honorably discharged on October 27, 1945, after serving his country with great pride and courage. He pursued a long and successful career in the airline industry and is currently retired. He lives on Long Island with his wife of over fifty years, Mary, and his two daughters, Susan and Linda.